Praise for J. Malcolm Garcia

"I don't know if he's unheralded, but there's a writer named J. Malcolm Garcia who continually astounds me with his energy and empathy. He writes powerful and lyrical nonfiction from Afghanistan, from Buenos Aires, from Mississippi, all of it urgent and provocative. I've been following him wherever he goes."

—**Dave Eggers**

"Garcia is an exceptionally powerful voice on behalf of the people about whom he writes. As he illustrates the results of America's military adventuring, Garcia not only takes us to the physical space of the people who are the victims of our drone attacks, our bombs, and our bullets, but he also goes where few nonfiction writers have the skill to venture—he takes us inside their heads."

—**Dale Maharidge, Pulitzer Prize-winning author of** *And Their Children After Them*

"J. Malcolm Garcia is the keeper of forgotten stories. He is an invaluable witness and a compassionate observer of today's wars."

—**Fatima Bhutto, author of** *Songs of Blood and Sword: A Daughter's Memoir*

WITHOUT A COUNTRY

WITHOUT A COUNTRY

The Untold Story of America's Deported Veterans

J. MALCOLM GARCIA

Hot Books

Portions of this book have appeared in slightly different form in the following publications: *Guernica: A Magazine of Arts & Politics, Tampa Review, Latterly Magazine* and *The Massachusetts Review.* The Nation Institute for Investigative Reporting funded some of the research.

Hot Books may be purchased in bulk at special discounts for sales promotion, corporate gifts, fund-raising, or educational purposes. Special editions can also be created to specifications. For details, contact the Special Sales Department, Skyhorse Publishing, 307 West 36th Street, 11th Floor, New York, NY 10018 or info@skyhorsepublishing.com.

Hot Books® and Skyhorse Publishing® are registered trademarks of Skyhorse Publishing, Inc.®, a Delaware corporation.

Visit our website at www.hotbookspress.com

First Edition

10 9 8 7 6 5 4 3 2 1

Library of Congress Cataloging-in-Publication Data is available on file.

Cover design by Brian Peterson

Print ISBN: 978-1-5107-2243-9
Ebook ISBN: 978-1-5107-2244-6

Printed in the United States of America.

Dedicated to Olga Contreras
1967–2016

The rest is silence

I am from there. I am from here.
I am not there and I am not here.
I have two names, which meet and part,
and I have two languages.
I forget which of them I dream in.

—Mahmoud Darwish

Life is a relentless expulsion from where we come from and an ongoing deportation to alien realms. We are in exile and our greatest dream is to return to the lost land. It is the greatest dream because no matter how long our exile is going to last, the dream will remain. It is the greatest dream because when we finally care only for this dream, then our exile will be over.

—Franco Santoro

What's curious, what's absurd is that despite
the fact I save the messages and cries
from all my memories and from
every cardinal point
what's strange what's incredible is that despite
my bleak expectations

I don't know what the wind of exile is saying.

—Mario Benedetti

Let the punishment be proportionate to the offense.

—Marcus T. Cicero

Contents

FACEBOOK, August 4, 2015, 3:22 p.m.
Hector Barajas-Varela
Learning to be a better person thru errors. Far from being perfect. Deported in 2004-present. Life deportation.

Prologue

I heard about Jose Chavez-Alvarez by chance, just after my journalism career crashed in 2009, a casualty of the Great Recession. I survived five rounds of layoffs at a daily newspaper before the sixth round tagged me.

Out of work for months, desperate, I accepted a job as a groundskeeper at a country club for minimum wage. Emptying trash, cutting golf course fairways, raking sand bunkers. My life as a reporter began slipping away. I determined to hang on to it. When the country club closed for the winter, I had a few months to freelance and regain my footing. Until then, I used my half-hour lunch breaks and the hours after work to pitch story ideas to editors.

Initially I thought I'd write about homeless Iraq and Afghanistan war veterans, a topical subject, good for the holidays when readers are interested in the poor. I had been embedded as a reporter in Afghanistan and knew people involved with social service nonprofits that worked with homeless vets.

"You really ought to do a story on deported vets," one social worker told me.

I had no idea that non-citizens served in the U.S. military, let alone that veterans were being deported. My contact gave me the name of Hector Barajas-Varela, an Army veteran and recovering alcoholic and drug addict who was deported to Mexico in 2004. He crossed back into the United States illegally a short time later but was caught and deported again in 2009. He then started a support house for deported veterans in Tijuana nicknamed the Bunker.

My contact also passed on the name of an immigration lawyer representing a Pennsylvania veteran facing deportation, Jose Chavez-Alvarez. According to a brief on his case, Chavez-Alvarez had sexually assaulted a fellow soldier while she was so drunk she was barely conscious. After the assault, she'd had trouble sleeping and interacting with other soldiers and was later diagnosed with post-traumatic stress disorder.

During his court-martial in 2000, Chavez-Alvarez said, "I just want to apologize to my entire platoon . . . and I hope someday, you know, they allow me to redeem myself for what I did wrong. [I] apologize to my entire chain of command, Army, and if [the female soldier] was here, I would like to apologize to her."

In the summer of 2012, nearly ten years after his release from prison, with no other crime on his record, Department of Homeland Security agents came to his house and arrested Chavez-Alvarez, imprisoning him for potential deportation as an aggravated felon. A 1996 law, the Illegal Immigration Reform and Immigrant Responsibility Act, calls for the deportation of immigrants convicted of crimes that meet the definition of an aggravated assault after they have been punished for their crimes by serving time in prison.

The law applies to an immigrant who served at least a year in prison (in most cases) and can be applied weeks, months, even years after his release. In addition to such serious crimes as murder and rape, a great many other offenses resulting in a prison sentence of a year or more can meet the definition of an "aggravated felony" and lead to deportation.

U.S. Immigration and Customs Enforcement, better known as ICE, does have discretion over whom it refers for removal. But the law does not permit any discretion on the part of immigration judges, who may not take into account a defendant's military service or any other mitigating circumstances once he has been convicted of an aggravated felony. The act can be invoked against an individual at any time. Complicating matters further, non-citizens do not have the right to a government-appointed lawyer, though they may hire their own if they can afford to.

No one, it seems, considered how it might affect veterans like Chavez-Alvarez who lived in the U.S. legally but were not yet citizens. Deported veterans include those who joined the military and those who were drafted. The military doesn't appear to encourage them to become full citizens, despite their willingness to die for this country. Many of them came to America as children, brought by relatives who left them no say in the matter. Had they kept their noses completely clean, or committed a different class of crime, they would have been eligible to pursue citizenship, just like any other green-card holder. In some states, they would even have been allowed to pay in-state college tuition, just as if they belonged.

Veterans, I learned, have only one sure way to reenter the States legally. When they die, those not discharged dishonorably are eligible for a full military funeral in the United States. Unwanted alive, they can return home as a corpse.

Jose Chavez-Alvarez was detained and taken to York County Prison in York, Pennsylvania, not far from where he lived—a town called, ironically, New Freedom. It is August 2014, and he is now fighting deportation to Mexico, where he was born forty-two years ago and has not been since his mother brought him to California when he was two. His mother died when he was a teenager, and an uncle and grandmother raised him.

After I finished reading the brief, I wanted nothing to do with Chavez-Alvarez. The guy, I thought, deserved to be punished. And a sexual assault conviction would not arouse the sympathies of an editor, let alone readers. His case was not the vehicle to resuscitate my career. Stick with the homeless vets, I told myself.

Yet I could not get it out of my head that, while an American convicted of the same crime would also be punished, he would not be deported. Technically speaking, Chavez-Alvarez wasn't facing double jeopardy. He was detained because immigration authorities thought his court-martial conviction fit the conditions laid out by the 1996 law to deport him. To a layman like me, however, Chavez-Alvarez was being punished twice for the same crime, simply because he was an immigrant. Had his uncle or grandmother, both U.S. citizens, adopted him after his mother died, he too would have been a citizen. It was just by chance he wasn't. Just by chance he faced consequences for his conviction that he otherwise would not have. I didn't need to like him to question why people who joined the U.S. military were not given citizenship and the entitlements citizenship provides. The minute they made the bargain to be willing to die for the United States, why were they not considered American?

In December 2014, I submitted a request to York County Prison to interview Chavez-Alvarez. As I waited for approval, I left for Tijuana to meet Hector Barajas-Varela.

Time Served*

D ecember 8, 2014. Tijuana, Mexico.
Hector Barajas-Varela wakes up at 8 a.m. in the former auto repair shop that serves as the home of the
Deported Veterans Support House. He sleeps in what had
once been a bathroom but is now storage for donated food
and clothes, stacked on overburdened plywood shelves.

The narrow space is just wide enough for his Army cot,
and although the room has no ventilation, it does allow him
privacy. He uses a thin bath towel for a door. Through the
towel, Barajas-Varela can see the gauzy outline of 60-year-old
U.S. Army vet Oscar Leyva in the front room, beginning to
stir on his cot. Leyva has diabetes and has difficulty walking.
Otherwise, he would stay on the second floor with me and
another vet from the U.S. Army, Alfredo "Al" Varon Guzman.

*Author's note: The names of Jose Chavez-Alvarez's children, as well
as that of the deported Marine mugged in Tijuana, have been changed
to protect privacy.

Camouflage military caps and photos of jet fighters and one of President Kennedy hang on the warped paneled walls in the room Guzman and I share. Sleeping bags and blankets stacked in a corner spill over onto the white tile floor near a desk. A plastic dinosaur and a broken TV perch on a nearby barrel.

An adjacent room has been made into a dining area, a sink in one corner, a large round table in the other. Only when we eat does Leyva make the painful trek upstairs.

From the second-floor windows, I look out at wide empty streets. A shuttered bar a few blocks away overlooks a scattering of parked cars that stretch toward distant mountains and the United States border. At dawn fog had concealed the mountains but now the sky above them is a clear and cloudless matte blue, and the noises of a city rousing itself replace lingering shadows. A laundry opens its doors and street vendors push metal containers, releasing steam, staining the cool winter air with the odor of beef and onions and cilantro. Dogs patchy with mange follow them, pausing to sniff around the garbage container outside the support house.

Another vet, a Marine named Ramon, used to share the second-floor bedroom too, but then one afternoon in late October 2014, he disappeared. Day after day, I would read messages Barajas-Varela posted on Facebook:

> *Our brother Ramon is missing.*
> *We're looking for him.*
> *Looking for him in the Tijuana morgue.*
> *Looking for him in the jail.*
> *Looking for him in the streets.*
> *We have not found Ramon.*

About three weeks after his disappearance, a doctor telephoned Barajas-Varela. Ramon had been in a coma for nineteen days at a local hospital. When he woke up, he asked for Barajas-Varela.

Ramon told Barajas-Varela he had been mugged. Puncture wounds scarred his neck, and the back of his head oozed blood from open cuts. He remembered nothing about what had happened to him other than that earlier in the day he had drunk a few beers. He insisted he had not gotten loaded.

Maybe he had, maybe he hadn't. Barajas-Varela kept his opinions to himself. But later he told me that if Ramon went out and did things like drinking that put him at risk, well then, he made that decision.

Barajas-Varela had regretted some of his own decisions, too. After he was deported, he became involved with a church and found a kind of peace working in Rosarito, a town fifteen miles south of Tijuana, as a caregiver for retired American expats. He began helping deported veterans too, letting them stay in his apartment. Many of the veterans liked to drink, and Barajas-Varela had no rules prohibiting alcohol. He should have. The stress of working all the time while some of the guys around him were partying led him to start drinking and using drugs, a habit that had gotten him into trouble in the Army and one he thought he had kicked. For five months he stayed on the streets drunk and high. Some nights he crashed in shelters. He saw how shelters had programs and did not tolerate the use of alcohol and other drugs. When he cleaned up, he determined to start helping deported veterans again, but this time with structure, expectations, and outcomes.

His efforts remain a work in progress, the hurdles immense. Being deported fucks with you. Nothing prepares you for it. Guys are depressed, in culture shock. They feel like they have no world. Home is just one border crossing away, and they can't go there. It tears at them, they get desperate. He knows quite a few people who have been killed. They got involved in drugs. They got into fights. They pissed off guys involved with criminal syndicates.

Who knows what happened to Ramon or why. Ramon didn't know or wasn't saying. Neither were the docs. They just discharged him to Barajas-Varela. But Ramon's injuries had jettisoned him into a paranoid world of Biblical prophecy. He paced the floors, muttered Scripture to himself: *Beloved, do not be surprised at the fiery trial when it comes upon you to test you, as though something strange were happening to you.* He complained of a negative "attitude factor" in the support house conspiring against him. What did he mean? He didn't know. He wanted to leave. He felt persecuted. By whom? He didn't know. He fell back on Scripture again: *Having a good conscience, so that, when you are slandered, those who revile your good behavior in Christ may be put to shame.* Barajas-Varela placed him in a church shelter.

The next morning, I arrived and assumed Ramon's cot. Jars of peanut butter, a box of Ensure, a pair of black shoes, and a box of candy crawling with ants had been wedged beneath it. On top of the cot, a sleeping bag partially covered a pillow stained from the cuts on his head.

"You might want another pillow," Barajas-Varela said.

Q: Were you friends with Specialist Chavez before he forcibly sodomy—sodomized and indecently assaulted you?
A: Yes, I was.
Q: Would you have considered him a good friend before those incidents?
A: We were friends. I worked with him. I knew him. I trusted him. He—he was the first person—first good person from what I knew of him and other people liked him and he was the first person I knew and he helped me out when I got here.

Q: Did you trust him?

A: Yes, I did.

Q: Are you friends with him now?

A: I really don't know him like I thought I knew him so I can't honestly answer that question anymore.

Q: How do you feel about him now?

A: I really—I really don't know what to think of him any-more 'cause he's like a stranger. I don't know him.

> Court Martial Record
> Chavez-Alvarez, Jose J. Spc.
> Camp Casey, Korea
> 20 November
> and 12 December 2000

January 28, 2015. York, Pennsylvania.

Jose Chavez-Alvarez sits in a chair, facing me and the closed glass door behind my back. Outside the door, a guard watches us, expressionless, shaved head, arms crossed, legs spread, a pistol strapped to his left hip. Light through a window spreads pale bars across the gray concrete walls above Chavez-Alvarez's head. He has short dark hair and glasses, and his nasal voice adds to the impression of a bookish university professor or a computer geek. He wears a green prison jumpsuit and sneakers. Because immigration detention is civil, the laws don't refer to immigration detainees as "prisoners" or "inmates." However, Chavez-Alvarez feels like nothing less.

He grew up just outside Los Angeles. He remembers his stepfather beating his mother. After she left him, mother and son moved from LA to Medford, Oregon, and back again. He attended school and helped his mother every summer picking grapes, green beans, and zucchini while

other six-year-old boys joined Little League. He would
wake up each morning and make strong coffee. His mother packed their lunches in paper bags. They spoke Spanish
but every now and then he would throw in English words,
"Good morning" instead of "buenos días," to help her learn
the language. She used to say, Come here, let me talk to
you. You do good in this country and you'll get anything
you want.

In 1987, when he was 15, a jealous former boyfriend shot
and killed his mother outside Fresno. A sheriff told his uncle.
Chavez-Alvarez was home at the time watching his younger
sister and brother. His aunt and uncle came by the house at
eleven that night. You're staying with us now, they said.

He contemplated suicide after his mother's death. At
night, he would get in his '64 Mustang and drive down a
rough patch of road he knew, shutting off the headlights and
accelerating. Whatever happens, happens, but nothing ever
did, so he considered a more direct route. He sat in the garage one afternoon with a gun. Sat. Thought about it. Then
his younger brother walked in and asked him for a ride to
baseball practice. What are you doing? his brother said.
Nothing, he said, and put the gun down.

Talking about it now, he cries.

A year after his mother's murder, his uncle helped him
apply for a green card, no different in some ways than applying for a driver's license. Chavez-Alvarez thought it made
him a citizen.

In June 1991, after he graduated from high school, he enlisted in the U.S. Army for the job training. He was the first
in his family to join. He first wore his Class A standard uniform when he finished basic training. Jacket, tie, and pants.
Looking at himself in the mirror, he thought his mother
would have been proud.

What will you do if the U.S. goes to war with Mexico? his uncle asked him.

Chavez-Alvarez laughed. He knew he would not be going to Mexico.

At the support house, minutes after a Barajas-Varela-imposed 8 a.m. wake-up, Barajas-Varela, dressed only in a white tank top and shorts and running a hand over his shaved head, wanders barefoot and somnolent past Leyva, who is now sitting on the edge of his cot, disheveled from sleep. Barajas-Varela grabs a broom. He sweeps, back and forth, back and forth, his body falling in rhythm to the tempo, the broom diminutive in his large hands. He yells upstairs, in a voice higher than I expected for someone his size, telling Guzman to get up.

Chores. Barajas-Varela believes in chores. The routine of chores. Feels it helps reinstall the Army discipline they once all knew so well. Guzman, however, isn't keen on reliving that part of Army life. He remains in bed as long as Barajas-Varela lets him, but I get up. Watching Barajas-Varela sweep, I feel compelled to do my part and begin mopping the bathroom.

No, not compelled. More like stepping back into a routine that had only recently been broken. Among other things, I cleaned bathrooms at the country club, as did my co-workers. They swabbed the floors with soapy mops and finished in minutes. I took much longer. I scrubbed, man. Floors, sinks, toilets. Got on my knees. I wanted my bathrooms to shine, to stand out from the rest. Distinct. Proof of my qualifications to do something more demanding. The supervisor would then show his appreciation, recognize my abilities, and promote me accordingly to an administrative position.

He didn't. I was part of a faceless crew cleaning bathrooms. No more, no less, no different.

I wonder if Barajas-Varela is engaged in a similar effort to assert himself beyond his circumstances. When he finishes sweeping, he sits at a desk draped with an American flag and turns his computer on to his Facebook page. Shelves behind the desk hold photographs of Barajas-Varela as a paratrooper in the Eighty-Second Airborne Division. He stares hard at the camera, almost as if he's issuing a silent challenge. Army strong.

I stand beside him as he posts messages. The posts range from greetings:

"Good morning everyone! Have a beautiful morning!"

To angry declarations:

"Deportations destroy lives, break up families."

To updates:

"Working with the ACLU on a medical parole / humanitarian parole for Armando Cervantes, Deported Veteran that needs urgent medical care in the U.S. Any Deported Veteran interested in the ACLU working on their VA benefits inbox me."

In response, he receives so many "likes." So many thumbs up. So many encouraging comments.

"Saludos, brother."

"Keep the faith."

"Hang in there."

Do his posts make a difference? I don't know. No more, perhaps, than my attempts to clean bathrooms better than anyone else. Pathetic, really, but you have to try, or you're lost.

A sheet of paper taped to the wall by Barajas-Varela's desk lists the names of veterans who died after deportation:

Dardar Paye	Kosovo	Army
Manuel Castano	Gulf War era	Army
Ramon Acero	Vietnam	Army
Manuel de Jesus Castano	Germany	Army
Hector Manuel Barrios	Vietnam	Army

Hector Barrios, a Vietnam veteran, lived in Tijuana. I decide to stop by the small house where he rented a room. A friend of his, Jesus Ballesteros, meets me on a sidewalk nearby, next to a red pickup that Barrios used to sell secondhand clothes from. I consider the narrow street, the house across the way with its leafy terrace and the sounds of water splashing from hoses in the driveway. Small boys scamper on the hot concrete, watering plants.

Jesus takes me into the room Barrios rented. It can't be more than nine by ten feet. A bed with a pink comforter takes up most of the space. At the foot of the bed, propped against a dresser mirror, is a large piece of cardboard with more than a dozen photos of Barrios. Several appear to be in Vietnam, outside tents with green Jeeps in the background. Barrios looks gaunt. He has a full black mustache, his tired eyes alive with an inviting smile. I sense that sleepless nights have grooved the wearied lines in his cheeks.

A green military jacket hangs from a coat rack and desert camouflage caps decorate the paneled walls. I notice a wrinkled newspaper clipping of Barrios as a young man, playing soccer, next to a calendar with an angelic portrait of Jesus. A photo of the pope is tacked crookedly to one side.

Barrios was born in 1943 and moved to the U.S. when he was eighteen. He served in the Army from 1967 to 1969. In 1968 he was sent to Vietnam, where he suffered head wounds in combat. He earned the National Defense Ribbon, the Vietnam Service Medal, the Vietnam Campaign Medal, and the Army Commendation Medal. But the honors did not relieve the pain of his injuries, and he began using heroin. Barrios was deported from the U.S. in 1999 for possession of marijuana. His addiction to heroin continued in Tijuana.

"Every day incoming fire, everything, fighting—you didn't know if you were going to come back home," he said in an interview with another reporter before his death. "It changes one's life. It changes everything. I came back crazy."

He always talked about Vietnam, Jesus says. How his commander died in front of him. They had been very close. They promised each other that if one of them got hurt, the other would bring him in. Barrios kept his promise.

"He had a big heart for people," Jesus continues. "He never mistreated anyone."

Barrios continued using heroin, however; he developed respiratory problems and died April 21, 2014. His family considered sending his body to the U.S. Despite his deportation, he remained entitled to a full military funeral since he had received an honorable discharge. But because the U.S. had thrown him out, his family buried him in Mexico and maintains his room as he left it.

"No one sleeps here except his ghost," Jesus says.

If you Google Hector Barrios, you'll find photos of deported veterans standing at attention beside his coffin, the black and yellow insignia of his unit—the First Cavalry Division— adorning the funeral home walls. Army veteran Fabian Rebolledo, a close friend of Barrios, was among those in attendance. He also suffered from war, Jesus tells me.

I meet with Rebolledo in Las Playas de Tijuana, in a house cluttered with unpacked boxes of clothes, stacked suitcases, and a bed, about a half-hour bus ride from the support house. The salt-air-rusted fence separating Mexico from the U.S. rises not far from his home. The brown cliffs of scorched mesas climb above a valley to the east while the sunset burns the pounding Pacific in bright orange hues.

Rebolledo chases a friend's collie out of the house and shows me in. He has on a blue Adidas sweatshirt and jeans. Like his friend Barrios, he has an inviting smile and an easy laugh, yet he speaks without betraying much emotion. He has a wrestler's build and moves easily within the maze of boxes. A thin mustache traces a dark line beneath his nose. He sits in a chair across from me, an American flag behind him. "Yes, sir," "No, sir," he responds to some of my questions, slipping into Army-think. He sits in a high-back chair facing me. I sink into a sofa, weak springs buckling beneath the cushions.

Rebolledo spent his early childhood in Cuernavaca, Morelos, south of Mexico City. His family's cramped house had two beds, a table, and a stool. A thin wood porch wrapped around the house. He and his parents and five brothers and sisters shared the beds. In the summer they slept outside on palm leaves, the early luster of warm mornings waking him. He would get up and fetch water in buckets hanging from the stick he balanced over his shoulder.

His oldest brother and sister moved to Los Angeles when he was eleven. A year later they paid for his father and another brother to come over. The following year, 1988, they sent for thirteen-year-old Fabian.

California. It was so big, he recalls. The buildings. The expressways. The expanses of land and houses and shopping malls that stretched for miles until they were so far away they shimmered uneasily on the horizon. At school, American students would say, Hey, you little motherfucker. He didn't know what they meant. He could not speak or pronounce English, but he listened and slowly began to understand.

His father worked construction and restaurant jobs. His mother sewed for a tailor. Rebolledo began washing dishes at a restaurant in Almonte when he was ten. He still remembers the address, 12050 Magnolia Blvd. He doubts it's still there.

He graduated from high school and enrolled in community college but dropped out to help his parents. He found work in farmers' markets. Sold shoes and boots, silly belt buckles, watches and sandals. Worked construction. In 1994, he became a permanent resident through a petition his father filed to adjust his immigration status.

That was a high. There were lows, too. A girlfriend broke up with him and he bought a beer to cope with his broken heart. He liked it. Liked it too much. He got wasted all the time. I need to do something, he recalls thinking. I'll end up in an institution, rehab, or the cemetery. In 1997, he enlisted in the Army. For the discipline. To answer the question, "What am I going to do with my life?" He was 23.

First stop after he enlisted, Fort Sill, Oklahoma. As soon as he stepped off the bus a drill sergeant started screaming. Maggots! he yelled. Rebolledo liked it. The sergeant's sweaty face, his snarling mouth. He saw the shouting as an act, something funny. He enjoyed the rush of hurrying to obey a command. Even now, as he thinks of it, his heart quickens. Push-ups, sit-ups, running. The shooting range. The hand-grenade field. Road marches. Twenty klicks. Sometimes it was raining or snowing, hot or cold or windy. Okay, weatherman, he would say to himself. Okay, bring it on. The sergeant yelling in your face, spitting in your face. Rebolledo bore it all, digging it, defying it. He never quit.

After thirteen weeks, he volunteered for Airborne School. What the hell? It paid $150 a month more. He was attached to Charlie Battery of the Eighty-Second Airborne Division and trained as an assistant gunner.

He can't remember specifics from his first jump out of a C-130. He was the third jumper. His legs shook. Hell, his whole body shook, heart in his throat. He thought he'd puke. He fell like a sack of weights before his chute opened, jerking him up like a yo-yo. He just had a few seconds to figure out where and how to land. Pull a strap and hope to come down softly. Took a while to learn.

When he hit the ground on his first jump, he didn't get up for a little bit. Good thing he had Kevlar to absorb the jolt. But when the shock wore off, he gloried in the feeling that he had fallen through the sky. He still remembers all of it. If he had the opportunity to do it now, he'd do it, do a jump despite his bad knees. Just last night he had a dream that he had jumped out of an aircraft, falling through all that sky.

In 1998 he met his wife, Bertha. Her niece was a friend and sometimes when Rebolledo called her in California, Bertha would answer and they would talk for hours. Within a month, he proposed to her over the phone and then paid her a visit. He thought she was pretty. Not supermodel pretty, but pretty. Soft skin, long black hair, black eyes, a nice body. They married the next day. He's like that. When he wants something, he doesn't second-guess himself. He goes out and gets it.

In February 1999, his battery was deployed to Kosovo. He had not paid attention to the war there. He had assumed he would be sent to Kuwait to deal with Saddam Hussein in Iraq. He packed his duffle. Bertha, pregnant at the time, returned to California to live with her parents.

Kosovo morphed into a bad dream. Rebolledo had not been overseas long when the Red Cross notified his unit that his wife had miscarried. I'm sorry, a captain told him. You have an hour to pack up and go home. Instead, Rebolledo walked to his tent and played dominoes. When his captain checked on him, Rebolledo told him, It's no good to go back. How good will I be watching the news of all you here? The baby won't come back whether I stay or go.

You're a bad motherfucker, the captain said.

He imagined who his child might have been in the face of innumerable horrors he saw as he patrolled Pristina, the capital of Kosovo, and swept the area for land mines. An uncontrollable anger crept up on him.

A sniper shot him in the leg one afternoon while he patrolled a corn field. Six shots from a semi-automatic. He thought a branch had hit him but when he stepped forward, his leg couldn't support his weight and he collapsed. He was evacuated to a hospital in Moldova.

At times the war overwhelmed him. Seeing the country all blown to shit, himself almost with it. Kids all fucked up. To him it wasn't human that people would do this to one another.

He felt helpless and lashed out. He beat up a soldier calling out for his mother and hugging his rifle. Hey, get the fuck up, Rebolledo said, and punched him. Straighten the fuck up.

His sergeant reported him. He was demoted, but a week later he was given his rank back, and he returned to the field more aggressive than before. He didn't take shit from anybody. What do you want now, man? he would say if he felt challenged. His only thought: stay alive. Like this one time he found a Serb trying to blow up a municipal building. The kid ran off before he could catch him. Little fucker rigging C-4 explosives. That sort of shit drove Rebolledo bat shit. Be alert, he would remind himself. Stay alive.

His commanding officers knew what Rebolledo could do with his anger. They would ask him to "give a little correction" to captured Serb soldiers. That meant covering their faces and beating the shit out of them. Then leave them in a heap on a road or some village for the Kosovars to finish off.

Don't do it, man, his gunner told him one night when Serb prisoners were turned over to them.

Who the fuck are you to tell me what to do? They're orders. If you don't like them, you know who you can complain to.

Eventually, he did stop. It got to be too much. Beating them up with his rifle. Kicking them. Afterward, he'd lie down and think that what he was doing was wrong, but he rationalized that it was just an order. Protect the mission. He felt further and further removed from his family. He called his wife every night until he had nothing to say to her and then he stopped calling. When his unit was ordered home in September 1999, Rebolledo didn't want to leave. His life was in Kosovo, not the U.S. But he had no choice. He returned to Fort Bragg, feeling as if he had landed in a foreign country. Too accustomed to being in the field among dead bodies, he slept outside. He got wasted all the time and cited for drunken driving. But drunk or sober, he was home. In March 2000, he received a general discharge and returned to civilian life. Four months later, his wife gave birth to a son.

Rebolledo found work as a security guard. In 2005, he got back into construction and also received another DUI. He dreamed of Kosovo, of dead babies. His temper flared. Yet he met all his familial obligations. He built a construction business, bought a house. He put food on the table, money in the bank. He would eventually seek help from the Department of Veterans Affairs for post-traumatic stress disorder (PTSD).

The Great Recession broke him. Three construction jobs canceled. He owed $5,000 a month for a warehouse where he stored his equipment. His trucks were repossessed. He had to sell the house.

In May 2007, Rebolledo was charged with felony forgery for attempting to cash a $750 check that he said he got for doing a stucco job. He was given probation. Authorities arrested him again three months later, this time for driving with a suspended driver's license as a result of his DUIs, a violation of his parole. He was sentenced to sixteen months in prison and came to the attention of immigration. He was released after eight months and turned over to Immigration and Customs Enforcement (ICE) for removal proceedings.

The immigration officials transferred him to a detention center in El Centro, California, in 2009. His wife divorced him, and the following year he was deported to Mexicali, Mexico. He had no money. Only his prison clothes, gray on gray sweats. On the bus ride to the border, a guard told him, You're a vet, right? So am I. OK, you didn't hear this from me. Check it out. You have seventy-two hours to get back into the States before your residency card is canceled.

In Mexicali, Rebolledo called his sister. She spoke to their father. He met Rebolledo in Tijuana and brought his residency card. Crossing back into California, Rebolledo told a border patrol officer, I was in the Eighty-Second Airborne.

I'm a Marine, the guard said. Come on, come on, you can go, I don't need your ID.

Living with his parents in LA again, Rebolledo worked construction. For two years, no problem. Then in January 2012, a police officer pulled him over for speeding near a Carl's Jr. He had no license, no state identification. The officer brought him into the Baldwin Park Police station and ran his fingerprints. No warrants, but his prints were sent to ICE.

About six weeks later, six ICE agents showed up at his parents' house. Six-thirty in the morning. Rebolledo got out of bed to answer the door. Squinting. His parents standing behind him. The sun barely up, the houses of the neighborhood slowly revealing themselves within the fading darkness. Nothing else. No neighbors about. The noise of a car somewhere far off.

Step out a minute sir, one of the agents told him. Are you Fabian?

Yes.

Do you have ID?

Rebolledo gave them his card from Veterans Affairs.

Where were you deployed?

Kosovo.

Really? I was in Pristina.

Really?

I was with the 379th.

I was with the 505th Engineering.

Can I see your DD214?

Rebolledo showed him his discharge papers. The officer said that two other officers with him were veterans, too. He walked a few paces away from Rebolledo to confer with them.

I can't deport a vet, Rebolledo overheard him say.

What do we do? one of the officers said.

No one spoke. Rebolledo heard their shoes scuff the concrete as they shifted their bodies, not saying anything. Heads down, glancing at one another. Thinking.

Say he wasn't here.

They gave Rebolledo his DD214 back.

Sorry, you're not who we're looking for, the first officer said.

A month later, about six-thirty in the morning again, Rebolledo's mother woke him up. ICE is here, she said. Sure he would be taken in this time, he hugged his parents goodbye. He dressed in a T-shirt and jeans and met the agents at the front door. He showed them his VA card. They consulted amongst themselves as the previous agents had, returned his card and apologized for bothering him.

But on the morning of June 24, 2012, his veteran status no longer mattered to the half-dozen ICE agents who confronted him at his parents' house. Seven in the morning. He was dressed and preparing to pick up his son at his ex-wife's. A trip to the mall to buy the boy some clothes topped his agenda.

Today is not your lucky day, one of the ICE agents said.

They escorted Rebolledo to a white van. He was held eight hours before he was deported to Mexico with twenty other men. He was the only vet. He got out of the bus and stood in line to cross into Tijuana. About four in the afternoon. The sun blazing, his handcuffed wrists sweating in the heat. A border patrol officer caught Rebolledo's glance at him and pulled him out of line. He pushed him against the bus and shouted,

You think you're fucking tough.

Yeah, I do, Rebolledo told him.

The officer punched him in the stomach.

You're just another fucking immigrant.

Leave him alone, an ICE agent said. He's going out.

Fuck all of you, Rebolledo said.

I'm sorry, the ICE agent said.

Later, local news stations interviewed Rebolledo and six other deportees at a hotel where they had pooled their money to rent a room in Tijuana. A woman walking past the hotel saw them being interviewed. Two days later, she noticed Rebolledo on the street and stopped to speak to him. He told her his story and she offered to let him stay at her home until he got situated. He eventually met Hector Barajas-Varela and lived with him in Rosarito for about seven months helping other deported vets.

Rebolledo no longer receives his military pension, and no longer receives physical therapy for leg and back injuries he suffered jumping out of planes. At first friends, family, and people supportive of deported vets sent him donations of $20, sometimes even $50. But now he hasn't gotten anything in months. People get tired of donating.

The house he lives in now is falling apart. The ceiling leaks. Mildew stains the cracked walls. He has agreed to repair the damage in exchange for not paying rent. He points to fresh smears of drying cement as evidence of his work. Not a good way to live but decent for Tijuana, Rebolledo says.

At night, he puts on a DVD for company and falls asleep to the voices of Mexican actors he doesn't know. Some days he helps a neighbor. An old friend from California might be here next Monday or Sunday. He'll bring canned food. Day by day, Rebolledo gets by.

I leave Rebolledo's house and catch a taxi back to the support house. The rolling streets outside my window stretch up into mountains, cinder-block homes casting long, slanted shadows down the steep streets.

My phone beeps, signaling I have new email. One message is from the lawyer of Jose Chavez-Alvarez. My request to interview Chavez-Alvarez has been approved. I lean back and stare out of my window. Chavez-Alvarez is no Fabian Rebolledo. No Hector Barrios, either. They saw war. It fucked them up. In Barrios's case, the conviction that led to his deportation—possessing marijuana—is legal now in some states. No, Chavez-Alvarez is not them. But like them he violated a varnished view of life and its self-serving, clichéd rhetoric where every soldier is a hero. Our "support the troops" mantra, passing these days for armchair patriotism, has no room for exceptions. We punish those who violate the mythology. We throw them out and move on; to new heroes and new bumper stickers.

> Q: And did the incident affect your ability to do those things that you—you did before the incident?
>
> A: Yeah. Yes, it does.
>
> Q: Such as?
>
> A: I—I just—I'm—I've been trying to go down range a lit-tle bit more lately, but immediately afterwards I tried to go down and I don't like going down there 'cause guys come up to you—I have—you know, my space. I don't like people coming up to me. I don't like my back up to the wall, but I don't—I also don't like to know that there's some guy behind me and there's no one else around me. I don't like being left by myself without someone I know. Now I hang out with just mainly females. And usually they're always with me. They always watch me to make sure, you know, that guys don't come up to me 'cause I don't like that.

> Court Martial Record
> Chavez-Alvarez, Jose J. Spc.
> Camp Casey, Korea
> 20 November
> and 12 December 2000

Chavez-Alvarez's Army division was stationed in Germany. He rode bicycles along the Rhine River and up steep hills with ancient monasteries at the top. He sent his grandmother $600 every month. In 1995, he received an honorable dis-charge and re-enlisted.

Chavez-Alvarez met the woman he would marry at Fort Sam Houston in San Antonio, Texas. She was studying to be an X-ray technician; he was attending physical therapy assistance school. She'd see him just hanging outside his barracks. They smiled at one another, joked around, hung out as friends until they became something more than friends. In 1996, the same year that Congress passed the Illegal Immigration Reform and Immigrant Responsibility Act, they married.

His wife's family hated him at first. She grew up in a community of white farmers. A Mexican man and a white woman, not something that went down easy. Her maternal grandfather refused to acknowledge Chavez-Alvarez. He'll come around, Chavez-Alvarez said, and he did.

After their marriage, they had two children, boys, both born in the U.S.

Neither Chavez-Alvarez nor his wife was aware of the 1996 immigration law any more than they were of most laws passed by Congress. The Army didn't question his citizenship when it gave him a second honorable discharge in 1997. Once again, he re-enlisted. Once again nothing came up about his status. Fill this out and you're good to go.

In 2000, on his third deployment, Chavez-Alvarez flew to South Korea to help set up a field hospital. On August 11, he and several other servicemen and women went out drinking at the Pleasure Dome, a soju club in Tongduchon, north of Seoul. Sometime between 10 p.m. and 5 a.m., Chavez-Alvarez and a female soldier left the club and returned to their barracks. Chavez-Alvarez then walked the soldier back to her room.

The next day he called his wife and told her he'd had sex with a woman in his unit the night before, and that she was now claiming he had raped her. He swore he had not. His wife had never felt so betrayed, so lost. She screamed into the phone. She wanted to die.

When he's not on Facebook, Hector Barajas-Varela, often wearing his military dress blues, a red beret cocked to one side of his head, attends meetings about immigration, drops in on churches, recruiting them to support deported vets, and holds interviews with media outlets from Tijuana and San Diego among others. He reminds me of a Chicago ward boss rallying the neighborhood for a particular cause. Barajas-Varela laughs at the comparison. Chicago. The States. Like a faint memory, he tells me. Then on the skyline of Tijuana he'll notice a Wal-Mart or a Kentucky Fried Chicken and it all comes back to him.

Barajas-Varela remembers growing up on his grandfather's farm in Zacatecas. The old man raised beans and at night told Barajas-Varela ghost stories about witches casting spells. When things got hard, his grandfather would take off for Colorado and work as a field hand.

Then, just like that, Barajas-Varela left his grandfather's world. With his parents he moved from Mexico to Compton in Los Angeles County when he was seven. His aunts and uncles lived there. It seems to him now that he always spoke both Spanish and English, although he knows he didn't start speaking English until he came to California. His family applied for and received residency. Only when he was arrested years later would Barajas-Varela realize that he was not a citizen.

His father cut lawns, collected cardboard for recycling, and performed any handyman jobs that came along. He saved enough to buy a house in a neighborhood where the Barajas-Varela family was the only Mexican family. They thought they had left the problems of the barrio behind. But they hadn't. Their car was stolen, house burglarized.

The dangers of the street were not limited to his neighborhood. High school seemed like one big gang. Between 200 and 300 kids would throw down on each other. He laughs about it now, the insanity of the violence. He doesn't know how many times he was beaten up.

In 1995, Barajas-Varela joined the Army to get away from the gangs, from Compton. He liked wearing the uniform, liked the way people looked at him. Even his homeboys: Damn, Hector, you doing good, dog. He was honorably discharged in 1999 and re-enlisted. Stationed in Texas. He drank heavily. El Paso. Right on the border with Mexico. A lot of drugs. He started abusing cocaine. He was processed out of the Army in November 2001, with an honorable discharge because of a DUI.

Three years later he was deported for shooting a gun from a car in Compton. Barajas-Varela denies he was the shooter. He says he and a friend were doing drugs, his friend got paranoid and pulled out the firearm. The police, however, fingered Barajas-Varela. He wouldn't rat on his friend and took the rap.

In prison, he heard about people being deported, but never thought it might apply to him until an immigration hold was assigned to his case. He represented himself to spare his family the expense of a lawyer. He fought his deportation for a year before he gave up.

You can appeal if you want, an immigration judge told him, before he handed down a twenty-year sentence that would not allow Barajas-Varela to return to the States before 2024.

Barajas-Varela stayed with his grandparents in Zacatecas before moving to Tijuana to be near the border and his family. But
he didn't feel near enough, so he crossed back into California illegally. He got involved with a Los Angeles chapter of Banished
Veterans, a group advocating for deported servicemen. He attended meetings, handed out flyers. He got a construction job
with a salary of thirty-one dollars an hour. Union roofer. Doing
well, too. Met a woman, had a daughter, Lilliana. But when he
rear-ended a car driving home one night, the police ran a check
on his name. This time a judge deported him for life.

The transcript of Chavez-Alvarez's court martial is a le-
galistic court document describing a horrific sexual assault.
The dispassionate tone and almost clinical detail make for
disturbing reading.

> Q: Do you recall meeting with LTC [name blacked out] re-
> cently?
> A: Yes, I do.
> Q: And what, if any, diagnosis did you learn she made re-
> garding your situation?
> A: I forgot what it's called now, but it's like post-traumat-
> ic stress syndrome, I believe. It's after someone goes
> through something traumatic for them that—it occurs.

> Court Martial Record
> Chavez-Alvarez, Jose J. Spc.
> Camp Casey, Korea
> 20 November
> and 12 December 2000

After he brought the female soldier back to her barracks,
she "vomited six to seven times and lay unconscious on
the bed. The accused was aware that [female soldier] was

unable to give consent due to her incapacity by intoxication." Nevertheless, according to the transcripts, Chavez-Alvarez had sex with the soldier, who "began to squirm around on the bed in protest as she realized what was happening to her."

The next morning Chavez-Alvarez provided two sworn statements to military police denying that he had had physical contact with the soldier. When the police told him that the soldier had accused him of rape, he admitted to having sex with her.

He was charged with rape, a charge he denied. The prosecution agreed not to pursue that charge if he would plead guilty to issuing false statements, to committing adultery and sodomy—defined by the military as "unnatural carnal copulation with another person of the same or opposite sex or with an animal." He did.

A military court sentenced Chavez-Alvarez to eighteen months in prison. He began his sentence on December 13, 2000, at Camp Humphrey in South Korea. After about four weeks, authorities transferred him to Fort Sill in Oklahoma, where he served the rest of his term.

While he was imprisoned, Chavez-Alvarez sought clemency. "My wife had sought legal assistance to file for a divorce because of the emotional strain my mistake placed on our marriage," he wrote in the conclusion of his appeal. "She has since decided to give our marriage and myself a second chance. To help us out we are going to seek marriage counseling to help get our marriage, lives and family back to where they should have always been. I have already lost my military career; I don't want to lose my marriage nor my family."

The Army declined his request.

The behavior of Chavez-Alvarez that night in Korea repulses me. I understand why people would think, Look at what he did. Deport him. Fuck him. He's an immigrant. He's not one of us.

Yes, I get it. Sometimes I wonder why I continue reporting his story. Who cares what happens to him? Why should we? Yet as a soldier in the Army he swore allegiance to the United States, not Mexico. Had he committed treason, he would have been tried as an American, not a Mexican. Had he died in combat, he would have been buried as an American, not a Mexican. How, then, is he not a citizen?

Only a cognitive disconnect could allow us to put people in uniform and not treat them as our own. I don't underestimate the pain Chavez-Alvarez inflicted. I don't pretend to know what it is like to be sexually assaulted, and I hope I never do. I offer him no excuses. But I also don't excuse the set of values that exploits our reactions to criminal acts only to perpetuate new suffering, by deciding that a person who served in the U.S. Army is not one of us.

At Fort Sill, Chavez-Alvarez lived in an open dorm and worked in the kitchen. He was released after thirteen months for good behavior on February 4, 2002. Because he had 726 days of unused leave, his period of service continued to January 30, 2004, when he received a dishonorable discharge. He returned to Pennsylvania, where he registered as a sex offender, which he thinks brought him to the attention of immigration authorities. He found work as a landscaper and then as a delivery driver for a florist. He and his wife stayed together. They talked. They said, We have kids. We'll work things out. There were a lot of late night conversations, but the marriage fell apart anyway. In 2005, they divorced.

The years after passed without incident. Then, in the spring of 2012, agents with the Department of Homeland

Security stopped at Chavez-Alvarez's house in New Freedom, Pennsylvania. He was at work. His girlfriend answered the door. After the officers identified themselves, she called him. He returned home and found two SUVs and a small van parked outside his house.

A Department of Homeland Security agent asked him for proof of citizenship. He asked his girlfriend to look through a safe in his bedroom for his military discharge, anything that might prove he was a citizen. She found only his green card.

The agents told him he would not be arrested. Instead, he would receive a letter to appear before an immigration judge. He never received the letter. About three weeks later, at 6 a.m. on June 5, 2012, he was arrested and charged with being deportable as an aggravated felon because of his guilty plea to sodomy in 2000. He was taken to York County Prison. Immigration authorities later charged him with being deportable for allegedly committing "two or more crimes involving moral turpitude."

In Tijuana, with the morning well past the 8 a.m. wake-up, Al Varon Guzman wanders downstairs from the second floor of the support house and opens the refrigerator. A month before my arrival, he flew from Bogota, Colombia, to Tijuana to volunteer at the support house. His stomach protrudes against his baggy shirt, his face drawn and sharp, etched with illness. If he is ever allowed back into the U.S., Guzman would make an appointment at the VA straight away for treatment of his ascites, a fluid buildup in the abdomen brought on when the liver stops functioning properly. After the VA, he would visit his children and grandchildren. He'd also apply for Social Security. He lost it when he was deported. All the money deducted from his payroll checks, gone too. Nada, nothing. Zero. Then he would return to Colombia. He would not remain in the U.S. Jobs for people his age, 56, are limited. In the U.S., he would be just another immigrant.

"Damn, this is nasty," he says, staring in the refrigerator and speaking in a distinct East Coast accent that reminds me of Brooklyn.

"I told you yesterday it was bad," Leyva says.

"I have to process my day," Guzman says and shuts the refrigerator door.

"You have to process your whole week," Barajas-Varela tells him.

Guzman slumps beside me on a couch. Silence—other than Barajas-Varela pecking away at his laptop. I take notes, stop. A heavy lethargy settles over us, similar to the complacency I felt at times at the country club. A kind of dejected acceptance that says, This is all life's going to be from now on. I became accustomed to emptying trash, staining benches, cleaning up fallen tree branches. Friends said, If this is the best you can do, you must not have been a very good reporter.

They weren't mean, they were scared. They knew that what happened to me could happen to them. There but for the grace of God, blah, blah, blah. They didn't want to feel vulnerable. I don't blame them. To avoid being vulnerable meant you had to blame the other guy, not some intangible economic forces beyond comprehension that could crush you too.

You must not have been a very good reporter.

I began to agree. It was my fault. Must be. I was doing something wrong. I was a bad person. I stopped sending out resumes, accepted my fate. I fell in step with the mindless routine of the country club, completing tasks without thinking day after day until I no longer thought about the future, about other options. I thought only of going home to sleep.

The same kind of inertia is insinuating itself here. What can a deported vet do in Tijuana? Washing cars nets about seventy-five cents an hour. Call centers hire for about the same rate. Support from families fills the financial void but does not fill the time. Only sleep does. But then you wake up. What then? Sit on the sofa. Wait. But for what? Nothing. Wait for the sake of waiting and to finally fall asleep again.

"Fucking Raiders are beating the Forty-Niners," Leyva says, reading sports news on his cell phone.

"How much?" Guzman asks.

"Twenty-four to thirteen."

"Eleven-point lead, they're done."

Guzman was four when his parents brought him to the States from Colombia. He grew up in Bogota, New Jersey, an enclave of Colombian immigrants. In high school he met a girl, she got pregnant, and they married. They moved to Manhattan where his daughter was born. In 1977, he enlisted in the Army after a recruiter gave him the rundown on benefits. It sounded more secure than his body shop job

He served in Germany with the Army's Third Division. Beautiful, some of those German towns. Quaint. Castles and green lawns. Like out of a fairy tale. He liked bicycling along the Rhine River. His wife, however, did not like Army life. She couldn't speak German and felt confined to the base. So Guzman left the Army when his enlistment ended in 1983 with an honorable discharge; he returned to New York and started his own business, hauling freight at JFK and LaGuardia airports.

In 1988, he was busted for forging a $365 check, money, he says, a friend owed him. He pled guilty and was given probation. Nearly ten years later, immigration flagged him when he applied to renew his security clearance at the airports. After fighting the case for five years, he missed a court appearance; he was in the hospital for spleen and gallbladder surgery. Soon after, he was deported to Colombia.

It was just, Let's go. What don't you understand? You're leaving now, a guard told him. Only thing you're taking is your clothes.

"They didn't give me time to breathe," Guzman says. "No money, no nothing else. Nada, zero."

From Colombia he called his sister in Phoenix. I'm over here, he told her. I don't have this, I don't have that. She arranged to have a family friend pick him up at the airport and he stayed with them. They bought him clothes and helped him get his Colombian ID. He found jobs teaching English.

"I was honorably discharged and honorably deported."

Leyva sits beneath a bulletin board listing the week's activities, his hair still askew from sleep, a heavy mustache drooping around his mouth. He holds his cell phone in one hand and with the other hunts and pecks names of people he knows in the States into Facebook, asking them to "friend" him.

"What does it mean when someone says, 'I see you have my image?'"

"Who said that?"

"My ex-wife just sent me a message," Leyva says. "'I see you have my image.'"

"Her picture, probably," Al says.

"There ain't no picture."

"Then I don't know."

"I know people in San Jose and Las Cruces. I remember people from high school but I don't know how to friend them. I've not seen anyone from my family in six years. My mother's supposed to be coming in March. Maybe April."

Leyva served as an Army specialist from 1972 to 1975. He was stationed in El Paso, Texas, and got caught up in the drug scene along the border with Mexico. He started with pot and cocaine and then took up acid. His bunkmate from Flint, Michigan, used to bury the acid in Folgers coffee cans and ship it around the States.

After his discharge, Leyva moved to San Jose. He stayed clean two, three years, drove trucks and then relapsed, hanging out with the wrong people. A felony conviction for cocaine possession with intent to sell led to his deportation to Mexico in 2012.

He lived in Chihuahua and drank. Then he saw Barajas-Varela on TV and decided to put aside the bottle and join him in Tijuana.

"What're we having for dinner?" Al asks.

"Chicharron," Barajas-Varela says.

"Grease. Can't eat," Al says.

"Oscar can eat it."

"Yeah, with beans."

"Thanks for making me feel better," Al says.

Leyva tells me you can pay for a fake green card to cross back into the U.S. He knows a guy who sells them. In the States, a green card costs about $400. You come to Tijuana, and a coyote will buy it from you for $1,000. The coyote then puts someone who wants to cross into a motel, and they spend the night going through a box of green cards looking for one with a photo that resembles the guy who wants to cross. They memorize everything on the card, name, age, birthdate. Costs about ten grand.

"Who has ten grand?" Leyva says.

Q: Has [the incident] affected your duty performance at all?
A: Immediately coming back after everything happened.
   I was emotionally—I would be—I'd be trying to do my
   job and the next thing I know I'd be in the back room
   crying in the bathroom. And then SGT [name blacked
   out] he's like, you know, you really—I know what happened, but you need—you really got to, you know, put
   your foot in there and get back to your job. There's a
   mission that needs to be done.

> Court Martial Record
> Chavez-Alvarez, Jose J. Spc.
> Camp Casey, Korea
> 20 November
> and 12 December 2000

Chavez-Alvarez tells me he has been locked up thirty-one
months and four days without a bond hearing while his
immigration case makes its way through the courts. His confinement has been almost twice as long as the time he served
for his military offenses. He doesn't know when he'll get out.
He knows immigration detainees who give up, get tired of
waiting to appear before an immigration judge. I want to get
out, they say. I'm signing out. I won't fight it. One guy, after
two weeks in prison, signed papers allowing for his deportation. Enough, he said. I can't take it anymore. That guy
even had stuff pending that might have helped his case. He'd
been in York two years, eighteen months. Another guy said,
I just don't like people around me. He was shaking. Three
days later, he was placed in medical segregation. Then he was
deported. He was in York less than a month.

Barajas-Varela shuts his laptop just as his cell phone rings. He answers, listens, and nods his head.

"All right. As long as he doesn't cause any trouble."

He hangs up, says to no one in particular, "Ramon is coming here for a shower."

Al and Leyva look at one another but don't comment. Barajas-Varela takes some handwritten intake forms—name, branch of service, type of discharge, reason for deportation, date of arrival in the U.S., current address, current circumstances—and puts them in a briefcase should he run into any vets in need of his help. He walks into his room and gets dressed: T-shirt, jeans, black military boots, red beret. Leyva turns to Al.

"What'd Ramon do to get deported?"

"Barajas-Varela won't say," Al says. "You know Ramon takes clothes to dry cleaners."

"At least he's stylin'."

They laugh and then stop laughing when the front door opens and a thin man wearing shorts, dark sunglasses, T-shirt, and a baseball cap walks in. He hesitates, nervous. He glances around until he sees Barajas-Varela. He asks if he may take a shower, in a voice barely above a whisper.

"Yes," Barajas-Varela tells him.

"How long, sir?"

"Five minutes, Ramon," Barajas-Varela says. "You know that. Water is expensive."

Ramon walks past Al and me without a word. I notice the back of his head, his injuries still raw and red. I listen to the shower. Barajas-Varela gets back on his laptop. We wait. Five minutes come and go. Glancing toward the bathroom, Barajas-Varela calls Robert Vivar, a friend who had worked with Ramon in a call center. Robert was born in Tijuana in 1956 and came to the United States legally with his parents in 1962. He worked for airlines in Los Angeles and later in Las Vegas. In the late 1990s, he developed a drug problem. He was deported in 2003 for stealing cold medicine from a supermarket. He is not a veteran.

Barajas-Varela asks him to speak to Ramon and see what might be going on with him.

About a half hour later, Vivar walks into the support house, the glare of the sunny morning following him into the front room until the glass door covered by an American flag closes, cutting off the welding flare of light. He is a barrel-chested man with short gray hair and glasses and a well-trimmed goatee. Peering over his glasses, he looks at Barajas-Varela seated behind his desk.

"I'll put him up Friday and Saturday," Vivar says, "but then I have to talk to his people."

"See if his family will come down from LA and help him find a place."

"OK, but we shouldn't lose sight of our primary mission."

"We're not."

"Leave no man behind, Hector."

Vivar walks to the bathroom and shouts through the door to Ramon that he wants to talk to him.

Barajas-Varela picks up his briefcase filled with intake forms. He is going to catch a bus to Rosarito, do a veteran outreach.

"'Leave no man behind,'" he says. "We've all been left behind."

William, the younger son of Chavez-Alvarez, agrees to meet me one night at a Denny's restaurant in Mechanicsburg, a suburb a few miles outside Harrisburg, Pennsylvania, where a glut of blue signs on Carlisle Pike promote Super 8, Econo Lodge, Budget Inn, and TGI Fridays, Chili's Grill & Bar,

Chipotle Mexican Grill, the placid sameness of each option blending with the indistinguishable, illuminated blur of rush-hour traffic in the deepening evening.

A waitress seats us in a corner booth. In the booths around us, children look at menus like picture books and their parents reach over their shoulders to point out enlarged photos of hamburgers, shrimp, and apple pie à la mode. William orders waffles with a fruity syrup. He is sixteen and resembles his father in every way, from the tone of his voice to the glasses he wears. He tells me his earliest memory is of his parents' divorce. He and his older brother Andy would stay with their father in the summer and during school breaks and most weekends. His next memory is of camping. They'd hike into the Appalachian Mountains near a lake not too far from where his father worked.

He doesn't think about his father's arrest in Korea. His mother told him he had sex with a woman and got locked up. When he was arrested again by immigration, his mother called William and Andy into the living room and told them what had happened. William got scared. He was thirteen and didn't understand why his father was taken away. He still doesn't.

His father calls every night from prison. They talk about *Game of Thrones*. His father asks about his dog, Otis, a pug. Give him an extra treat. Keep him healthy, he says.

William doesn't like the prison. It's . . . well . . . he doesn't know. It's different. He gets pretty nervous when he's there. The guards stare at everyone. One time he saw his father laugh with a guard. They seemed to be friends.

When his father was home, they used to read together. Can't do that anymore. One time in school, William was studying Greek history. He had a question about a Greek god, he doesn't remember which one now. He thought, I'll ask Dad. Oh, wait. I can't. He's in prison.

William has told a few of his friends about his father's situation. It feels weird to talk about it. His brother told a friend who asked William about it. What's done is done. He can't help what his father did in Korea.

"If you were in my position," he asks me, "would you want your dad to leave the country?"

Deported Veterans Support House Outreach Intake
Name: Gonzalo Chaidiz, 67
Nationality: Mexican
Military branch: Army 1968-1971
Type of discharge: honorable
Reason for deportation: Assault
Arrival in the U.S.: When he was six
Current address: Horizon Rosarito Church, Rosarito,
    Mexico
Current circumstance: church no longer wants to house
    him

"He's a good guy and then he loses it," Pastor Armando Gonzalez tells Barajas-Varela. He leads us through a cafeteria to the back of the church where workmen clear rubble near a trailer. "But he thinks he owns the place. He saw a guy smoking and went off. He said, I don't want you smoking here. We took him to a halfway house and he assaulted staff. Maybe if he lived with people going through the same thing he is, it would help."

"Maybe we'll try him for a couple of days," Barajas-Varela says.

As the pastor and Barajas-Varela speak, Gonzalo Chaidiz walks into the church. He has on a winter coat, gray T-shirt, blue jeans, and sneakers. He wears glasses, and his short gray hair sticks up on his head like clipped grass. He carries a plastic bag filled with bananas and oranges. He offers Barajas-Varela a banana.

"The pastor wants you to come stay with us for a few days," Barajas-Varela says.

"But I have a job here," Chaidiz says, "cleaning a school. I make 200 pesos a month."

"That's like $20," Barajas-Varela says. "That ain't shit."

"I know, but it's something."

Barajas-Varela asks him to think about it. Chaidiz agrees.

"He needs help," the pastor says. "He's sad, sad."

Deported Veterans Support House Outreach Intake
Name: refuses to give name, age
Nationality: Mexican
Military branch: refuses to say. Does say he served in
    Vietnam
Type of discharge: refuses to say
Reason for deportation: Won't say other than he accrued
    27 DUIs.
Arrival in the U.S.: refuses to say
Current address: a convenience store he owns and operates
    in Rosarito
Current circumstance: his water has been cut off

We follow a stone path leading off the highway toward the convenience store. Picnic tables lean into the ground, and a vegetable garden grows in a patch of dirt off to one side, bamboo sticks supporting tomato vines.

Barajas-Varela has met with this man several times, and each time the man refuses to answer his questions.

"Give up," the man says. He sways in front of us, breath reeking of beer. He holds a clutch of water bills in his hands.

"Give up, Hector. You're not going to change a thing."

Deported Veterans Support House Outreach Intake

Name: Juan Montemayor, 59

Nationality: Mexican

Military branch: Army 1977-78. Joined after two friends
 OD'd on heroin. He didn't want to end up like them

Type of discharge: General discharge. Stationed in Texas.
 Arrested for transporting undocumented Mexicans
 across the border. Paid $700 to $1,500 per person. He
 spent 45 days in a military jail

Reason for deportation: drug possession crack cocaine.
 Deported in 2004, crossed back. In 2005 he was stopped
 for jaywalking by a police officer. Hey, don't you know
 how to cross the street? Do you have ID? The officer
 took his name and ran it.

Arrival in the U.S.: Doesn't remember. Just an infant

Current address: a trailer in Rosarito

Current circumstance: homeless

"You know Joe?" Barajas-Varela says.

Juan Montemayor scratches the hard, gray stubble on his face, his mouth collapsing around a few remaining teeth, crooked, tobacco-stained remnants, reminders of what else his calamitous choices have taken from him. He drops a trowel in a bucket. When we walked up, he had been applying cement to the wall of what appears to be an addition to a house. The job won't last beyond today.

"Joe? Yeah, he died of a stroke last week. I was going out to see him and found out." Montemayor steps back, examines his work and slaps on more cement. Hector watches him.

"One thing about surviving, if you come here with the same way of thinking you had in the States, you won't make it. You'll go back to that lifestyle. You got to look for work or start your own business. You got to deal or go to jail."

"Where're you staying?"

"I was with Joe at the beach for a while. Got soaked when the tides came in. Maybe I can stay with you, Hector?"

"You'll have to go through detox."

"I got bad for a while."

"We all do."

The next morning, I return to Rosarito to meet deported veteran Alex Murillo. He picks me up at a shopping center where Christmas trees had been arranged in front of a Wal-Mart. I think of Barajas-Varela's comment: The U.S. is like a faint memory. Then I think of Wal-Mart and Kentucky Fried Chicken and it all comes back to me.

Murillo is sitting in the passenger seat of a sedan that pulls up to the curb. At 37, he has black hair and an easy manner, liberally dropping the word "dude" into his speech. He introduces me to the driver, Harold, an Iraq War vet who moved to Rosarito to escape what he saw as the chaos of life in the U.S. "Who needs it, man?" he says. His hair is tied back into a thick pony tail, his pupils wide from the pot he has been smoking. I sense beneath his hippy-jive-love-peace-and-brotherhood rap the desperation of someone seeking something he won't find in Rosarito despite the expanse of calm ocean and the soothing taste of salty air and the wide, empty streets with cars slowly moving, and the sense that what he has left behind will catch up to him here. Later, Murillo tells me Harold has PTSD.

From the Wal-Mart, we drive past shopping malls and restaurants with steaming grills outside. Murillo wants me to meet another deported vet, Gerardo Lopez. Harold takes a side street, and we climb a hill and pull alongside a white stucco

house with a red-shingled roof. The three of us jog down a
set of steps to an apartment that overlooks the ocean. Music
blares from inside. Murillo knocks and the door is opened by
Lopez. His 21-year-old son, Marcus, is visiting him from the
States and stands behind him. Marcus is tall and thin, a con-
trast to his 41-year-old father's body builder's bulk. The elder
Lopez's shaved head and wraparound sunglasses lend an aura
of menace when he speaks, looking at me with eyes I can't see.

Marcus had not seen his father in years until Lopez
tracked him down on Facebook.

"I thought he was dead," Marcus said. "I got his Facebook
message and I thought, 'I guess he's alive.'"

Lopez said Marcus's mother had put their son out of the
house and he was living on the streets in Chicago. Lopez had
lived on those same streets. You know what you can get on
the street. You get shot out there. Happened to me.

"I sent him a bus ticket," Lopez says.

"Yeah, when I got here and he opened the door, I thought,
Damn, that's my dad. He's bald."

"I thought he was tall," Lopez says. "We played basketball. He won. I hooked him up with a girl. He handled it. I'm
proud of him."

Marcus shuts off the boom box and steps outside to shoot
hoops with Harold and Murillo. I take a seat on one of two
white couches spilling over with clothes from a toppled
clothing rack, metal hangers cascaded into a pile. Lopez sits
at a table covered with cigarette ash. He turns to me, offers
me a glass of orange juice.

"How much do you want to know?"

"Why'd you get deported?"

"I broke an off-duty police officer's neck."

In many respects, his life had been building to that con-
frontation. Lopez grew up hard after his family brought him

to Chicago. He was born in Mexico near El Paso, Texas. He remembers snapshots of his childhood, like the time he fell into a well and screamed until his family came running and hauled him out. Or the time he injured his left foot when he stepped on some burning wood. He remembers how he cried, and the days he was laid up with his foot wrapped in a fat, white bandage.

He crossed the border with his parents when he was three. They had visas and never looked back. They drove to Chicago where some aunts and uncles lived. The neighborhood was rough. A guy broke into an aunt's room one night shortly after they arrived. She shot him but didn't kill him.

He loved the skyscrapers downtown. There was a guy the press dubbed Spider-Man. He climbed Sears Tower. He remembers the lights at night illuminating the sky over Navy Pier. Lake Shore Drive. All that.

Kids picked on him. He didn't know English. His clothes weren't hip. His family had little money. He learned to fight back. He didn't get along with his father, whom he says was abusive. When Lopez got big enough, he beat his father's ass. Lopez left home after he graduated from high school. Hooked up with this girl he met at a Venture store. Cashier. Fresh off the boat from the Philippines. They had a baby, his first son, Marcus. But he wasn't ready to be a father. He saw other girls, pimped some of them out, and Marcus's mother got all jealous. Took out a machete one night. He called the cops, but they saw her and a kid and arrested him instead of her. Spent a night in jail. When he got back home the next morning, she had torn up all his clothes. She screamed some voodoo shit at him and told him the spell she cast would prevent him from ever being happy. She took Marcus to San Francisco.

Lopez had this friend, Alfredo, a Puerto Rican guy. He joined the Navy. Nice uniform blue and gold. Girls all on him. Lopez wanted in. He wasn't doing so good running the streets. In August 1995, he joined the Navy.

Boot camp in Chicago, then on to San Diego Naval Air Station. He loaded bombs with VS-35 Squadron. The Blue Wolves. They went all over. Diego Garcia, Hong Kong, Singapore, and Japan. He liked the adrenaline rush. Locking in the bomb. Putting bombs on a rack knowing sometimes a bomb will be dropped and explode somewhere, killing bad guys. He'd watch the planes leave. He was part of a five-man group. Part of something.

Then, while he was on a drill, he fell, broke a bone in his left foot. The doctors inserted a metal rod, and he was on convalescent leave. He performed light, limited duty, a pencil pusher cooped up in San Diego while his squad was out. Not what he signed up for.

He started staying out late, disregarding orders. In 1997, he received an other than honorable discharge—an administrative release from service for misconduct.

Lopez remained in San Diego and met the mother of his second son. He has not seen them in years. Then in 1998 he had his fight with the off-duty police officer outside a bar. Lopez says he held the officer in a headlock and broke his neck. The officer survived. Lopez was charged with felony assault but pled down to aggravated assault and was sentenced to a year in jail. The attorney didn't mention that a plea deal to an aggravated assault charge could get him deported. After he did his year, he never saw daylight in the States again. U.S. immigration authorities sent him straight to Mexico.

He was fortunate, he had someplace to go. A friend in Rosarito put him up until he got it together to get his own place. Now he works security in clubs. Kicks people out, holds them down on the sidewalk when they try to start something. Lots of fights. He has a busted knuckle to prove it. A busted knuckle and all he gets is $20 a gig. He started his own business detailing cars, hiring himself out as a personal trainer. Bartends, too. Sells what he doesn't need at swap meets. A survivor, a hustler. He knew if he made it in Chicago he'd make it here. Even if he had to do bad things, he'd make it. He wasn't looking in that direction but just saying. Sometimes, he tells me, you're left with no choice.

Murillo, Harold, and Marcus saunter into the apartment as Lopez and I end the interview. Sweat shines on them. Despite the cool ocean breezes, the heat from outside fills the small apartment, the stink of their exertion mixed with the salty sea air. Murillo wants to roll, eyes combing over each one of us, breathing hard from the basketball game but not even close to being tired, the impatient high-wire act of a guy who has time on his hands and doesn't know what to do with it.

We jump back into Harold's ride and roll downtown and park outside shopping centers filled with tourist trap trinkets. Plastic matadors, colorful piñatas, and ridiculously huge sombreros. Murillo walks through aisles like he's on a mission, leaving me little time to be tempted by tacky displays. We are back at the car in minutes and bop over to another shopping center, and another and another, Harold and I keeping pace with Murillo, stepping without pause, moving, doing something, anything, running from this fucking boredom, dude. Murillo is learning how to play the piano. Something to fill the time, break out of this deported box.

So broke, sometimes, he fishes off rocks jutting out of the ocean. Fills the time. A hook, a line, and clams for bait. Doesn't catch shit, but walking around on those rocks, good for balance, dude. He slows down when he sleeps. Dreams. Being back home in Phoenix. With his mom. She makes him breakfast. Kids running all around. He goes out skateboarding. Started that when he was 30. Midlife-crisis-thing. Then he wakes up. Shit.

We run out of shopping centers.

"What do you want to do, dude?"

"Let's go to your place, do this interview," I say.

"Yeah," Murillo says. "All right, dude. Let's knock it out."

Harold spins us off the main drag to a cluster of buildings just beyond downtown and pulls into the parking lot of a square yellow building. We get out and Murillo leads us into his studio apartment. Dishes all over the sink and stove. A desk strewn with papers and ash trays, a chair and sofa. An incomplete painting he has titled "American Mouse in Distress" lies on a faded recliner. It shows a Micky Mouse-like character saluting, the bones in his hand breaking through the skin. A knife sticks out of his back, blood drips from his heart. Murillo isn't sure what the painting means. Maybe something to do with what's happening in Iraq. He began painting in prison. To get out from behind the walls, dude, out of the box. Free his mind if not his body. It's all about getting out of the box.

Harold splits to wash his ride. Murillo gets on his computer and clicks on a movie. Planet of the Apes. The latest one. The phone rings. Murillo's oldest son on the other end. Calling from Phoenix.

"How you doing?" Murillo said to him. "How's school?"

Murillo was born in Nogales, the last one in his family to have been born in Mexico. He was an infant when his parents moved to Phoenix. He remembers nothing of his birthplace. He grew up as an American kid. He played baseball and basketball. Didn't care for soccer. He scored A's in grammar school and was on the honor roll in junior high.

"What's going on in school? What do you mean? . . . I thought you were getting good grades."

As a high school sophomore, Murillo started screwing up. Treading that line between dropping out or not. Spending too much time with his girlfriend. He did graduate but his grades had sunk so low he was ineligible for college grants and financial aid. His parents didn't have the money to send him.

In October 1996, after his girlfriend became pregnant, he joined the Navy. Quit screwing up, he told himself. Make your family proud, take care of the baby, and after your enlistment, attend college. Get into law enforcement. Something exciting.

"How's it gone down to C's, son? . . . Straight C's? That's a straight average. How are you going to get into college? What are you having problems with, son? You were getting A's and B's."

Murillo became a naval mechanic. He said he was voted honor recruit in boot camp and graduated top of his class in aviation school in Pensacola, Florida. He loved the Navy but hated it too. Loved the camaraderie, meeting other sailors from all over the United States, but he had a phobia of being swallowed by the ocean and floating away into nothingness.

After three months at sea, he returned stateside for a brief break before beginning a six-month deployment. He started drinking a lot then. Young marriage and baby all at once, away from his family. Twenty years old, he was just a kid. Maintaining equipment, working sixteen to eighteen hour days. The job wore him down.

His ship, the *George Washington*, returned to Norfolk, Virginia, in 1998. He drank more and more. He got popped on a piss test for marijuana. He was placed on restriction. One night, he cut his wrists with a razor blade. He doesn't think he wanted to kill himself. Maybe he did. Or maybe he just wanted out. He spent about two weeks in the psych ward. He spoke to a chaplain often and to a doctor a few times. The doctor jotted comments in Murillo's file. He doesn't know what he wrote any more than he understands how the doctor helped him. When he was released, he left the Navy in 1999 with a bad conduct discharge. He doesn't know if his bad conduct was his failed suicide attempt or his drinking. Maybe both. He thinks the Navy was particularly upset with the suicide attempt. It resented his effort for trying to destroy government property.

"I'm going to stay on you about your homework. Bring back A's and B's. More A's than B's. I have to stay on you . . . I know, son . . . I want to see you. How's your mother doing? I'm trying to get a job."

Murillo returned to Phoenix and continued drinking. His marriage, already rocky from his time away, worsened. He and his wife tried to make it work and had two more children but the marriage didn't last and they divorced. His drinking began costing him jobs: Home Depot, Cox Communications, DirecTV, he can't say how many jobs he lost. He couldn't pay child support. His wife would not let him see their children.

In April 2009, he found another job, the wrong job. He agreed to transport around 700 pounds of marijuana for a dealer and got busted in St. Louis. He was sentenced to thirty-seven months in the federal prison in Lompoc, California. While he was there, immigration flagged his name. In December 2011, after he completed his sentence, he was deported. A prison bus.

"I care, son, because I'm far away. You have to move forward. I messed up. I'm paying for it. You got to be a success, son. I see nothing but good stuff ahead of you if stay on those grades."

Murillo can still see himself getting off the prison bus that carried him from detention to to the San Diego/Tijuana border. It was 11 p.m. He had $120 hidden in his prison sweats, gray on gray, his only clothes. Guards unshackled his hands and feet, and he walked off the bus. Pitch black out, the air heavy. A guard gave him a cup of noodles, shrimp flavored. He got one phone call. He tried to reach his mother but the call didn't go through. He stepped forward, his left foot in Mexico while his right foot remained in California until he raised it, too, and crossed over.

He stayed with a cousin and then moved to Nogales. He didn't like it there, felt people held his "Americanness" against him. In September 2012, he resettled in Rosarito.

With the help of his family, Murillo started a satellite dish sales and installation company. He coaches football and freelances as a photographer and videographer. And there are his piano lessons, too. Still, he feels restless, bored. The box always closing in.

His mother brings his children down for visits when she can. They throw a ball on the beach until they leave. He watches them go, that fear he had of the ocean overcoming him, that feeling of being sucked into nothingness taking hold once more.

"Apply yourself a little more, OK, son? . . . All right. We'll web chat later? OK. Tell your brother and sister I love them very much. I love you, son. Bye."

He puts down his cell phone, slumps in his chair. He stares at the wall. He raises his head to the ceiling and covers his face with his hands. He digs his fingers into his forehead, and tears pour down his face beneath his hands.

"I just want to get back home, man," he says. His voice catches. He speaks barely above a whisper. "I just want to see my kids."

That evening, I stay in Rosarito with Victor, a friend of Barajas-Varela. Victor is a Vietnam vet and an expat. He was not deported. Barajas-Varela cared for Victor's father when he worked in a Rosarito assisted living facility.

Victor lives in an oceanfront house, the sound of crashing waves in the starlit evening and the rinse of salty air a sedative to the hot day. He gives me a room above his garage. Before I call it a night, he introduces me to his neighbor Louis Montanez.

Montanez speaks with a rat-a-tat patter that allows for few pauses. His smooth face, dark hair, and antic manner make him appear much younger than his forty-two years. We sit in Victor's garage, the door open to the night, the bugs dancing in the heat of porch lights, and Louis loops me into his head with this declaration: "I'm an American dude. I was a year and half old when I came to the United States. But I had to reconcile the fact that I'm a Mexican cat. I'm not a veteran. I played soldier as a kid. I watched the footage of bombs and blood and shit on TV and it was not to my liking. So I'm not a vet but I feel their fight because I was deported too. But people like Hector, they chose to do this, join the military. And then they get deported. What makes this real? You're taken, dude. Stripped of your life, man. All of a sudden the big unit, this large force, immigration, sucks you away. It was like, fuck, really? It's a different scene than anything you've experienced. I did commit a crime, a fucking burglary. I'd been in the United States twenty-six years. My mother's grandfather is French. Am I a French cat, too?

What makes this real? I went to prison, did my time. You take it. It's acceptable. You got caught. After you struggle through prison, they put you in a camp for deportees. I was sent to Eloy, Arizona. You're in the meat grinder. It's crazy, man. A crazy tunnel sucking you away. You step into another zone. You're being fed, no problem. Got a cot to sleep on, no problem. Just like prison. But they're saying, You're not us. I always thought I was. No, we have a hold on your freedom. What makes this real? You get your scope on other people, man, you meet other cats. 'I'm Steve whatever' and they say they're veterans. I didn't know what happened to them. You got a bunch of people, three to four thousand in my area. You have cubicles. You're in a cubicle. Holds X amount of people. Then they get shipped off. Another cubicle moves up the list. Then the people in it get shipped out. It's just fucking crazy, man. OK. I'm in Mexico. Then I meet Vic. I met him here in Rosarito. Oh, what do you do? and we get to know each other. I liked him like I did his father, Grandpa Vic is what I called his father. This is another maze I'm traveling through that will change my life. Grandpa Vic was getting sick. Vic took him to a senior citizen place. I go visit him. I got to meet Hector Barajas-Varela. He was working there, trying to survive, man. He cared for Grandpa Vic. We got to talking. He's a deported vet. Wants to go home. Me, I'm interested in the immigration deal. I'd just been deported. This was 2009. It's all one thing. It's all immigration. It's all part of the same fucking process. It's about family, man, and a good job. You had that there in the States and loved that. You fucked up but you did your time, but this process you're caught up in doesn't think that was enough. Now you're here. I'm trying here. I'm not just here and trying to live over there. You do that and you're not living. Still, your mind wanders to over there sometimes and you think, What makes this real?"

Andy, the older son of Chavez-Alvarez, is 18. Like his brother, he meets me at the Mechanicsburg Denny's one night, and, like his brother, his idea of dinner is that of a teenager. He orders French fries, nothing more, and soaks them with ketchup. He holds himself with more self-assurance than his brother and speaks carefully, considering his words. He, too, looks very much like his father.

He does not remember much about his father's court-martial. From time to time he would ask his mother, Where's Daddy? But the memory of that question makes him uncomfortable. Maybe that's why he doesn't remember much. He asked his father about it one time, his freshman year in high school. His father told him he slept with another woman and lied about it.

Andy had just come home from school when his mother told him that his father had been arrested by immigration agents. She did not know how long he would be in jail. She thought it might all be over by Christmas. She said his father was not a citizen of the U.S. If he wasn't a citizen, why did it take them this long to arrest him, Andy wanted to know. It never occurred to him his father wasn't a citizen. Why would it?

The whole thing was strange. His father was arrested the last day of school. Or the day before the last day, Andy isn't sure which. Right at the time he and his brother were to go camping with him. His mother said his father was thrown in jail for what he had done in Korea years before.

The first few times Andy visited his father in prison, he cried. He couldn't touch him. They were separated by glass. When he was first jailed, Andy and his brother could visit him for as long as they wanted until a guard told them to leave. Now, he can't stay for longer than thirty minutes. Nice guards let them stay longer, if no people are waiting. He and his brother split the time or take one visit apiece. Their mother sits in the waiting room and waves at his father when she catches a glimpse of him. When it's time to say goodbye, Andy and his father fist-bump against the glass.

It seems his mother has been more stressed lately. She gets angry more often. Andy lets her take it out on him. He understands why she's angry. Everything thrown at her. Every now and then he vents, too. He tries not to let it get to him too much.

Q: What are you doing to try and move past this event and move on with your life?

A: I'm trying—trying to go home. I've been trying to go home for a while now, since this happened. I just want to get back to my family. I've been going to church. Trying to get back into a church. Reading my Bible a lot and praying. Trying to hang out with my friends.

> Court Martial Record
> Chavez-Alvarez, Jose J. Spc.
> Camp Casey, Korea
> 20 November
> and 12 December 2000

At the San Diego/Tijuana border. The San Ysidro port of entry. Saturday. About 5:30 p.m. Already dark. Cars backed up for what looks like miles. The glare of countless headlights and border lights diluting the night with flaxen luminescence. Barajas-Varela in his dress blues, red beret tilted to one side of his head. He ironed his uniform early this morning. Still fits. A little tight around the stomach, not much. Oscar Leyva and Robert Vivar beside him. Barajas-Varela raises a bullhorn.

"I am a deported U.S. veteran." He demands that all deported veterans like himself be allowed to return home. He wants all these people heading into California to carry that message with them.

"Veterans are being deported. They served their country. Leave no man behind. Bring us home."

He talks on, reminds his listeners of the sacrifices soldiers make. Risking their lives. Leaving their families.

"Bring us home."

When he begins to lose his voice, he passes the bullhorn to Vivar, who repeats the message.

"Bring us home."

Static from the bullhorn bites into his words. The cars inch forward. Some of the drivers look at Barajas-Varela, Vivar, and Leyva while others wipe sweat from their foreheads and stare resolutely ahead over their steering wheels, the intensity of their stares suggesting they think they can move the stalled traffic through willpower. Vendors hawk their wares along the roadside. Plastic statues of the Virgin Mary. Christ on the cross. Bundled flowers. They take no notice of Barajas-Varela as he gives one last shout into the bullhorn, "Bring us home!" and turns to leave. The absence of his voice. As if he had never spoken. The quiet absorbed by the noise of so many idling engines.

This evening Barajas-Varela lies on an Army cot and calls his nine-year-old daughter in LA "Do you miss me?" he asks her. "I miss you." He has stripped out of his uniform down to his shorts and a white tank top. Tattoos arc across his back. His shaved head reflects the glow of the ceiling light. His thin mustache draws a dark line beneath his nose. He lies on a cot in his room, distracted by the noise of cars and the distorted music rising out of a karaoke bar next door. Dogs roam the streets toppling garbage cans. An American flag conceals the glass front door.

Through Skype video hookup, Barajas-Varela sees a Christmas tree his daughter has decorated. He tells her he wishes he could be with her.

"It's beautiful," he says of the tree.

Then the video connection shuts off.

"I can't see you," she says. "Daddy, I can't see you."

He taps his phone. She calls out to him but he will not see her again unless he reconnects through Skype.

Barajas-Varela has plans. A, B, C, and D. One plan, gather at the border with other deported vets and request asylum. Get an attorney ahead of time. Get put in detention. He can see the headlines: "Vets Not Allowed in U.S. Held in Jail." The worst case, they'll get deported again. Then it's on to plan B, C, D. Whatever it takes.

Twenty-seven hundred miles away from Tijuana, Chavez-Alvarez lives among the general inmate population of state and county inmates in York County Prison. Those guys aren't facing deportation proceedings like him. They don't give a shit. They know their release date. Immigration inmates don't. They can be held for years. The state and county inmates fuck with the immigrants, steal their shit. If a non-citizen inmate like Chavez-Alvarez retaliates, a judge will see the write-up. Oh, another aggravated assault, the judge might say, and just like that you're fucked, you lose your case.

Chavez-Alvarez reads a lot, blocks out the bullshit, day-dreams about his sons, about the camping trip they planned days before he was picked up. When he's not buried in a book, he works in the prison distributing clothes, bed rolls, and hygiene supplies to new detainees.

Some nights Chavez-Alvarez imagines a guard waking him at 3 a.m. Hey, you're getting deported today. That happened to one guy. 3 a.m. Get your clothes, shackles on, and he was off.

"Two honorable Army discharges mean nothing because of one night in Korea," he tells me. "One time in my life I made a huge mistake. I never did this again. It's hard to explain. I don't know what came over me. It was one night of extreme stupidity on my part."

One night. That's how he sees it. One night. He knows others see it differently.

Outside Barajas-Varela's room, Ramon paces. The church Barajas-Varela had referred him to could not or would not house him any longer, Barajas-Varela isn't sure which. It doesn't matter. He's back at the support house reciting Scripture:

Have mercy on me, O Lord; consider my trouble which I suffer of them that hate me, you that lift me up from the gates of death.

Leyva talks on his phone to a friend in the States. He says that when he came to Mexico he was always fucked up and didn't think about his deportation. Now that he has stopped drinking, he can't not think about it. An attorney told him that with an aggravated felony conviction, he "ain't got no action." The only thing he can do is wait and see if the laws change in a way that might allow him to return.

"I have an eighty-four-year-old mother and two grandkids I never see," he says. "It's not like I went to the United States and committed felonies from the start. I had a lot of good time."

Guzman gets on a computer and communicates with Facebook friends. Some nights he thinks over his life. How he's lived it. Angry for putting himself in this situation. The first few nights after he was deported he didn't sleep. He had never felt so lonely.

I jot down what Guzman tells me. He asks me where I will go when I leave Tijuana. Pennsylvania, I reply. When I met Chavez-Alvarez, I heard about an Iraq War veteran fighting deportation in Lancaster, Neuris Feliz. He had agreed to meet with me.

"Where will he go?"

"Dominican Republic. Hector told me of another veteran who got deported there. Hans Irizarry."

"Sucks to be him," Guzman says.

He taps out a cigarette and stands to smoke outside. I see the orange flare of the tip of Guzman's cigarette and the same sense of loss I had experienced at the country club overtakes me once more, as if it had followed me here to this other exile. Guzman's life, Leyva's, Barajas-Varela's, and the others are all connected to the lives of other people; they are more complicated than simply their definition within the penal and immigration systems.

When have we punished enough?

Now I'm Not a Hero

Early morning, January 2015. I am sitting with Neuris Feliz in the dining room of his Lancaster, Pennsylvania, apartment. Faded shades drawn, the gray light of an overcast winter morning barely breaking through. On his desk a horse-head profile embossed against the yellow shield of the First Cavalry Division that he served with in Iraq. Near it, a photo of Feliz in his Army uniform, an American flag behind him.

Three deflating heart-shaped balloons from his thirty-first birthday party the night before sag above our heads. A poster on the wall behind them reads, Live, Laugh, Love. Feliz looks younger than thirty-one. Black hair, wide brown eyes, a weary smile. Just he and his wife and a bottle of pink wine, a red ribbon slipping down it. Happy Birthday. Perhaps the last birthday he will celebrate in the United States.

"I live here," he tells me. "Hell, my favorite sport is football."

But he is not from here.

Feliz was born and raised in the capital of the Dominican Republic, Santo Domingo, with a brother and three cousins. Early in his childhood, his mother, separated from his father, left him with an aunt and moved to Spain and later Puerto Rico to find work.

He spent much of his time in the countryside of the Dominican Republic. So free. Not congested like Santo Domingo. He remembers canyons deep and wide, small wood houses, and all types of fruit. There were sheep, cows, horses, sugar cane, and coffee plantations. Clouds concealed the tops of mountains and fog descended across valleys at night with the stealth of ghosts. In the morning, he wore a jacket until it warmed.

In 1995, when he was eleven, Feliz traveled to Puerto Rico to rejoin his mother, who had returned there from Spain. He met his father for the first time. His father worked construction. His mother sent Feliz to him one night. His father called him a momma's boy. Something like that. Feliz threw a rock at him and fled back to his mother but his father chased after him and beat him up. His mother and aunt slapped him too. You don't throw rocks at your father.

Four years later, Feliz and his mother moved to Lancaster, where other family members had gone before them. The weighted mugginess of Pennsylvania's humid summers surprised the boy. The nineteenth-century brick buildings with their sagging wood porches looked ancient. He had never seen so many white people up close.

He attended summer school, enrolled in English as a Second Language classes. Within a year he'd learned the language well enough to participate in classes with American students. His aunt taught him multiplication, slapping his knees with a belt when he answered incorrectly. He fell in love with science. He wanted to be an astronaut.

He grew restless as he advanced into his teens, however, and school no longer captured his imagination. He spent his high school senior year clubbing and drinking. He didn't bother to attend graduation. If he could talk to the young man he was then, Feliz would tell him, If you lose your love for school, you lose everything.

The terrorist attacks of 9/11 refocused him. His country had been attacked. He thought of the United States as his country. No one had told him otherwise. In 2002, he signed up with the Army National Guard. Within a few months he went active.

"With me, it was, 'You want to join? Sign here,'" Feliz recalls. "I don't remember the recruiters saying anything about status. But they did ask for my green card."

He began his enlistment in March 2002. One year later in March, while Feliz ran a war-games drill lugging a 90-pound rucksack ten kilometers across the Kansas prairie, the United States launched the war against Iraq. Feliz didn't grasp that a war had started. That was part of being in the Army. Don't think. Do. He loved that. That sense of purpose. Just do. Civilians stopped and watched him when he walked past them in his uniform. How impressed they looked. He didn't know of anything to beat that feeling.

Feliz deployed to Iraq in 2004. A power generator mechanic in the First Cavalry Division, he landed in Camp Doha in Kuwait. Three weeks later, the division began a three-day drive to Sadr City in northeast Baghdad.

So many people on the street. The desert heat and dust. The convoy inching through jammed markets. Move, move! Get out of the way! the Americans shouted. Some soldiers from the 115th Battalion, including Feliz, bivouacked (set up a temporary encampment) at Camp War Eagle, later the site of combat with the Mahdi Army, an Iraqi paramilitary force.

Daily mortar attacks became the norm. Feliz rode in convoys and heard the gunfire, the ting of metal when bullets struck his vehicle.

For six months, he pulled guard duty six hours on, twelve hours off. Sometimes he directed vehicles driven by Iraqis entering the camp into a large concrete box that would contain a blast should the vehicle be wired for a bomb. If it blew up, so would he. Still, the war didn't seem real to him until one hot evening in April 2004, when Feliz stood by the camp's main gate and heard explosions. OK, he thought, another firefight. Then he saw a truck racing toward the gate. More vehicles came behind it, all of them carrying wounded. He heard someone shouting, "Medics! Medics!" He responded automatically. He and others of his squad put the injured on stretchers. Ankles, arms, legs, all shot up. Everyone running so fast. Seven or eight people died. He realized where he was. Iraq. In a war. Not a war exercise, but a real war. He told his pastor he had blood on his hands from trying to help the wounded.

Not long afterward an Improvised Explosive Device (IED) killed a close Army friend, Leslie Denise Jackson. She had worked in supply and drove back and forth between Camp War Eagle and Camp Muleskinner in eastern Baghdad. When her vehicle struck the IED, Feliz heard the explosion. He had no idea her vehicle had been hit until he got off guard duty. His squad leader told him. He couldn't believe it. She was only eighteen. He could not get her out of his mind. "I didn't join the Army for this," she would say every time a mortar hit a convoy and wounded soldiers had to be treated. Feliz saw the killing and dying was getting to her. For days after her death, he kept recalling her words: "I didn't join the Army for this."

He changed. No more "Don't think. Do." He talked back to his supervisors. He didn't complete his work. His superiors, he said, did not suggest he seek counseling, though an Army spokesman told me counseling would have been available to him at the camp. Instead, they allowed him a four-day leave in Qatar. From there, he spoke to his family and his pastor in Lancaster.

"He was depressed, crying," Cesar Melo, pastor of the Iglesia de Poder en Acción, or Church of God's Power in Action, said to me over the phone before I met with Feliz. "He saw parts of the body of his friend after the explosion. He didn't understand why we had to go to war. He didn't want to live. He wanted to go home."

When he returned to Camp War Eagle, Feliz assumed his old don't-think-do attitude. He told everyone he was OK. To all appearances, he was.

In 2005, Feliz re-enlisted just before the First Cavalry received orders to return to the States. Once in Fort Hood, Texas, everyone took a thirty-day leave. Feliz returned to Lancaster. He stayed drunk the whole time.

Back at Fort Hood and awaiting redeployment to Iraq, Feliz continued drinking. He did not seek counseling. He didn't think he had a drinking problem. He was just partying, glad to be back. But he couldn't keep himself out of bars. He didn't think he had a drinking problem. When they were on, he wouldn't let her out of his sight. He didn't want to be alone.

"I was very selfish, very possessive. I was running from my life," Feliz says, describing that time. "I felt very alone."

In May 2005, after a day of drinking, Feliz drove to his girlfriend's apartment at night. A guy stood in the parking lot waiting for her. He said they were dating. When she drove up, Feliz grabbed an ax handle from the trunk of his car and ran up on the guy as he was getting into her car. Feliz began slamming him with the ax handle. Swinging like a baseball player, hitting the guy four times on his right knee and ankle. The guy screaming and trying to shield himself, the girlfriend screaming, the guy half falling, half jerking himself into the car and slamming the door.

Feliz ran to his girlfriend's side of the car and cussed her out as she sped off. She had her two-year-old son with her. He remembers that. He doesn't like that he cussed around him. He was drunk and angry. He left his girlfriend's place, drove to a strip club, and drank. To this day, he says, he does not know why he had the ax handle or even how it got in his car. For protection, he thinks. But he cannot imagine from what.

That night the police questioned him at his apartment. He told them what happened in the parking lot and gave them the ax handle. The police left without detaining him. A week later, they called and told Feliz to come to the station for more questioning. He didn't. He didn't give a damn. Another week passed and the police called again. This time they told him to turn himself in. He complied. He still didn't give a damn. He just wanted to get past whatever was coming. He tells me now he could have asked the Army for legal assistance as an active duty service member, but instead he went with a court-appointed lawyer. He didn't care about the consequences.

Feliz pleaded guilty to aggravated assault. According to court records, the judge asked him if he understood that if he pleaded guilty, the United States could choose to "deny you the right to remain in this country, they might deny you the right to apply for citizenship and they could in fact deport you from this country. You understand that?"

"Yes, your honor," Feliz said.

The judge sentenced him to five years. He was twenty-two. Feliz says now that he does not recall the judge speaking to him.

"I just remember saying yes to everything," he tells me. "I don't remember much. I was just going with whatever they gave me."

When we spoke by phone, he reflected on his sentence.

"My lawyer wasn't that much of a—" he begins and then pauses. "He was court-appointed and didn't do much. He told me I'd get probation and then the day of sentencing he told me the DA was asking for four years. But really, I didn't care too much."

After Feliz told me about the ax handle assault, I spoke to psychiatrist Judith Broder, founder of the Soldiers Project, a national nonprofit based in Los Angeles that provides counseling for post-9/11 servicemen and women. She was not surprised by Feliz's post-deployment behavior.

A sense of alienation, reliving traumatic experiences, and anger can all contribute to drinking and drug abuse and other self-destructive actions, Dr. Broder told me. How much of this behavior has led Iraq war veterans to prison is unknown. Available information is woefully out of date. The most recent veteran incarceration data from the U.S. Department of Justice dates back to 2004, just one year after the Iraq war started. It found that ten percent of state prisoners reported prior service in the U.S. Armed Forces. A majority of these veterans served during periods of war but did not experience combat duty

Few people would dispute that soldiers are often ill-prepared to return to civilian life, and that lack of preparation can lead to problems, legal or otherwise. A 2008 RAND report, "Invisible Wounds: Mental Health and Cognitive Care Needs of America's Returning Veterans," found that 300,000 veterans who had served in Iraq and Afghanistan suffered from PTSD or depression. In addition, about 320,000 may have also suffered traumatic brain injuries.

Symptoms of PTSD include aggressive, hyper-alert behavior that is necessary for survival in war but creates problems in civilian life, Dr. Broder told me.

"Veterans talk about a 0-to-10 anger reaction," she said. "Their anger goes off instantaneously and escalates to 10 very, very fast. It is a combination of post-traumatic stress and being hyper-reactive to anything that constitutes a threat."

Such feelings may have led Feliz to put an ax handle in his car.

"Many veterans we see keep weapons at home," Dr. Broder said. "They keep them under the bed, in the car. They even bring them into therapy sessions. They sense danger all around. There's no on/off switch."

In 2007, while Feliz spent a second year in jail, the Army hit the switch on his military career. Unable to complete his second enlistment, he received a general discharge under honorable conditions.

As an inmate, he worked in fields picking potatoes. A guard on horseback, the butt of a .45 jutting out of a shoulder holster, watched him and the other inmates hoeing in time like slaves. From Iraq to prison. Treated like dirt. Pork served every other day. He vied for space with fifty other inmates in his cubicle. First-time offenders, probation violators. Bunk beds along the walls. He had to be discerning. Each inmate had certain ways, particular habits. He learned them to avoid arguments, fights. Chess, Scrabble, a player accuses another player of cheating. Someone stares at someone else. Game on. Testosterone way high. Don't get into it. Don't look. Not your business. That was Feliz's attitude. He read, spoke only when spoken to.

He had a lot of time to think. What he did, what he could have done differently. Not drink, not fight. If only he hadn't come home from Iraq and partied. He took a class on cognitive intervention and his love for learning returned. He resolved to live responsibly and for himself.

In a journal he wrote:

One day my most desired wish was to meet death. Fly
away and disappear into the firmament. I wanted to dive
into the most remote places I could build in my mind. I
hated people. I hated myself. I couldn't stand to witness
another sunrise every dawn. Agonies abounded in my
deepest entrails.

Another entry reads:

Grab a man, place him in a lonely and empty space, let him
be alone, just by himself. Take his friends, family, his most
beloved belongings, his most beloved people. Take his de-
sires away, aspirations and ambitions. Erase his memories,
his past and even dreams. Who would this man turn to
when he's lost it all?

With time off for good behavior, Feliz served three years and
one month in prison. After his release in 2009, he returned
to Lancaster where he took a job at Tyson Chicken. The
following year he enrolled in Thaddeus Stevens College of
Technology. He started dating Carolina Martinez. In 2011,
he returned to the Dominican Republic to meet her family.
His life, he felt, was on an upswing.

Feliz stayed two days in Santo Domingo before he flew to
San Juan, Puerto Rico, to visit his mother, who had returned
there after he joined the Army. As part of their routine procedures, airport customs officers checked his name as they did
for all passengers and became aware of his felony conviction.
They took his passport and green card and detained him for
nine hours before they gave him a summons to report to an
immigration judge in Philadelphia.

Since then, Feliz has been fighting to remain in the United States. His Lancaster attorney has argued that as defined under immigration law, "aggravated felony" differs significantly from how the Texas penal code defines it and therefore does not apply to Feliz. In other words, Feliz's crime does not meet the definition of a crime of violence as interpreted by the board of immigration appeals and federal courts, he said.

Feliz tries not to think about the complex, Rubik's cube set of arguments and counter arguments that will determine what country, the U.S. or the Dominican Republic, he will call home. He has gotten on with his life. He graduated from college in 2012 and accepted a job with a graphics company. He married Carolina in 2013. However, nothing he does feels certain, secure. He doesn't know what his future will hold or even where he will live it.

I leave Pennsylvania to meet Feliz's uncle and cousin and his wife Carolina, who was visiting her family in the Dominican Republic. I want to see what Feliz faces if he has to return to a place he no longer considers home. Deported veteran Hans Irizarry meets me at the Santo Domingo airport late on a humid Tuesday afternoon. He stands slouched to one side waiting for me at the end of a hall. He moves toward me when we see each other. He has a roll to his walk that at times blossoms into a strut. A dragon tattoo encircles his left arm. He wears a baseball cap tipped down the left side of his head. A 38-year-old badass.

I got in touch with Irizarry through the Deported Veterans Facebook page. He speaks Spanish. I don't. I'll need his help with translation when I meet Feliz's family.

I rent a car, and from the airport we drive to the house of Luis Milanes Mendez, 78, and Yeimi Mendez, 37, an uncle and cousin of Feliz's. He lived with them as a child after his mother moved to Spain.

They remember him as a normal, calm boy. Humble. He did what he was told. He played baseball and enjoyed swimming. When he moved to Puerto Rico to be with his mother and later to the United States, Yeimi felt his absence. She had regarded him as a younger brother.

Feliz called Luis and Yeimi when he joined the Army. They were so happy, as proud as any father and sister would be. For him to be part of the US military, the most powerful military force in the world, well, that feeling compared with nothing they had ever known.

From Iraq, Feliz wrote to his mother. She sent letters to Luis and Yeimi, and they forwarded them to other family members. He said he missed them all. He wrote about hungry Iraqis and how they reminded him of the poverty in the Dominican Republic. These thoughts made him think of his family and he grew sad and lonely.

Feliz spoke very little about Iraq during his phone calls after he returned, Yeimi said, not even about the death of his friend. He had always been quiet, but the pronounced silence that hovered around him could be felt even over the phone. It was like he was missing a part of himself.

Luis and Yeimi did not know what to think when they heard Feliz had been charged with assault in Texas. They didn't understand. They didn't know him to be violent. They felt even more confused about his situation now. Why, they asked, is he facing deportation for a fight? They don't know U.S. immigration law, but how can anyone say that's fair? He risked his life for America and now it wants to toss him out?

If he is deported, of course we will take him in, Luis tells me. You have to be careful of everything, he would warn Feliz. You have to know where and what to say, what to do. Everyone carries a gun. Don't get into a fight. Here, they'll kill you. Don't try to be brave. It is dangerous. Step on a

person's foot, sorry, and they kill you. That's how bad this
country is.

When Feliz called recently, Luis and Yeimi told him not
to give up. OK, he said. They did not hear from him again for
weeks. That silence again.

Already, a part of him had been removed.

Irizarry and I leave the Mendez house and drive to the home
of Feliz's in-laws to meet his wife, who was visiting her family. We had not gone far when two police officers, in what
Irizarry later described as a typical encounter, stopped us.
Irizarry showed them his expired Army identification.

"You're American? You're the boss," one of the officers
says.

"No, you're the boss," Irizarry says.

"We're here to protect you," the officer continues.
"Anything you can do to help us, we'll take."

"What can I tell you? I'm short of money."

"Anything you consider good, we'll take."

"I need money from you," Irizarry says.

The officer steps back. There are two kinds of cops in the
Dominican Republic, Irizarry tells me as we leave. Traffic
cops during the day, like these guys, but after dark it's the
badasses. At night, Irizarry won't stop for the police. The
night cops will tell you to get out of your car and take it.
Now, you're walking. Now you're a target.

"I've had police fuck with me," he says. "They see the tattoos and earrings. 'Oh, you're a deportee. We're looking for
some criminals. You look like one of them. Where're you
from? How long have you been here?' What has saved me is
the military ID."

The Dominican Republic wasn't always like this. Irizarry
was born in Santo Domingo in 1976. Those were different

days, he says. Cops didn't shake you down. No bars on house windows to keep out burglars. He could sit in front of his house and not worry about gangs. Every time it rained, he stood outside and played in the puddles or under a gutter overflowing with water. Now kids don't do that.

After his mother and father divorced in 1990, his mother moved to New York City with thirteen-year-old Irizarry, his older brother and younger sister. Some aunts and uncles were already living there.

They moved into an apartment at 125th and Broadway. Irizarry learned English easily. After school, he and his sister walked home and he would cook dinner. His mother and older brother worked for a tailor late into the evening. When he turned sixteen, Irizarry got his residency card. He assumed that made him a citizen, although he didn't really think about it one way or the other.

He attended college and studied computer science. Bored, he dropped out. His mother got on him. What are you going to do with your life? He didn't know. But he always liked war movies. The more he thought about it, the more he believed the Army would offer him a future. He certainly had no sense of direction now. So, on a whim in 1997, he walked into a recruiter's office and asked how to join. They did not ask about his status. Four weeks later, he was in boot camp.

Irizarry and I stop outside a multi-storied house painted in tropical hues of yellow and orange. It stands behind a sun-dappled concrete wall. Feliz's wife, Carolina Martinez, opens a heavy metal door in the wall to let us in. Yard cats trail after us into the kitchen and up a flight of stairs. We sit near a balcony enclosed by bars. A photograph of Carolina's father in a military uniform hangs on a wall. A maid brings us orange juice.

Carolina, 29, has known Feliz since they were children. They lost touch but met again in Pennsylvania when she was visiting her sister. He had been out of prison for six years by then. She found him to be atypical of most Dominican men. He was not macho. He seemed very open-minded. He did not hang out with other women. He wanted children and to grow old with a wife.

After they married, he showed her photographs of dead bodies in Iraq. Very ugly things. He told her Iraq was not easy. He had nightmares. He kept saying he wanted to go back. Before they married, she said, she had not seen that part of his personality that had been affected by war.

Carolina was in Lancaster when customs officials detained Feliz in Puerto Rico. He had called her that morning before he left Santo Domingo for San Juan to visit his mother. Carolina worried when she didn't hear from him the following day. She wept when he finally called and told her what had happened. She still cries about it. She tells herself everything is going to be OK, but she can't be certain.

"Listen, since you'll be talking to him, tell him to go on the run," Irizarry tells her.

"He'll never do that."

"If he doesn't and gets sent back, he'll regret it."

"I don't want him over here, to trust people here. He needs to be hip to street talk. He doesn't know it."

"Tell him to run."

She shakes her head. If he gets deported, he will use his military knowledge to survive, she told me. But that may not help him, she concedes. People here pick fights for anything. He doesn't know how things are.

"Run," Irizarry insists.

Again she shakes her head no, a sad smile crossing her lips. Impressed, perhaps, by Irizarry's persistence. No, not run. The U.S. government should give Feliz a chance. It should look at all the years he has not been in the Dominican Republic. It should look at his military service. He fought for the United States, after all, not the Dominican Republic.

Irizarry, too, was married as a U.S. soldier, tying the knot with a girl he'd met in 1998. He also was deployed to Kuwait as part of Operation Desert Fox, a four-day bombing campaign on Iraqi targets led by the U.S. and the United Kingdom. He unloaded tanks, M-16s, missiles. He spent six months in the desert seventeen miles from the Iraqi border. He carried a gas mask with him everywhere, including the latrine. He almost got himself killed when he drove an armored vehicle into a minefield. He stopped, looked, saw mines all around him and backed out the way he'd driven in.

He returned to the States in May 1999. That June, while he was stationed at Fort Stewart, Georgia, he notified his sergeant that he was taking his pregnant wife to the hospital for a checkup. His sergeant told him if he wasn't back on base in fifteen minutes, he would take his rank. Irizarry, just back from Iraq, wasn't taking this shit, and went AWOL. He and his wife left for New York. Two months later, Irizarry turned himself in to the Army. In 2000, he received an administrative discharge, which he appealed. It was later upgraded to general discharge under honorable conditions.

While the upgrade resolved one problem, a more immediate issue, employment, remained. He didn't like his supervisors hovering over him like he needed hand-holding. He didn't think like them. He behaved as he had in the Army. Tell him to do something, he did it. Just like that, done. What's next? His co-workers would mess with him. "Why are you working so fast? Who you trying to impress?" Or, "I didn't tell you to do that, Irizarry."

"You did, too."

"Watch how you talk to me, Irizarry."

"Fuck you," and he was gone.

Irizarry and his wife divorced in 2003. By then he had two daughters to support. In and out of work, he wasn't making any money. The bills piled up. In 2004, he ran into an old high school buddy, a drug dealer. If you need money, all you got to do is pick up a package and you'll make $800, he told Irizarry.

Irizarry didn't ask what would be in the package. When he picked it up, the police were waiting for him. The package held two ounces of heroin. Irizarry was arrested but got out on bail. He was due to face a judge who had a reputation of sentencing everyone who appeared before him to fifteen years to life. So Irizarry jumped bail and fled to Florida, where his father had immigrated. About a year later, the police caught him. He was extradited to New York and sentenced to four and a half to nine years. He served three and a half because of time served in Florida waiting to be extradited.

"Do you think a good father would have done what you did?" I asked Irizarry as we drove back to his apartment. "I mean, transport dope?"

He stopped the car. He turned and faced me. Speaking in a measured tone, a tight grip on his anger.

"Listen, you cannot tell me what is a good father. You do anything for your kids not to starve. I did everything it took. It was an easy way out. It was stupid, selfish. I went to Iraq. I was a hero. I got caught with drugs, now I'm not a hero? If I hadn't been caught, would I still be a hero? A lot of people have done stupid things and have not been caught. They're lucky. It was a mistake, a stupid, dumb, desperate mistake. You don't know what people go through. I explained to my daughters, 'I'm here, I got deported. I did a crime involved with drugs. It was the wrong thing, and that's what happens if you break the law.'"

In 2007, while he was still serving his sentence, Irizarry received a summons to appear before an immigration judge. According to trial transcripts, the judge said he could not give Irizarry a break.

"I do appreciate your service to the country. I mean that quite sincerely. . . . But because of the drug convictions, the way the Immigration Laws are written, I'm not—I have no discretion. I'm not allowed to consider things such as how long you've lived here. Your family ties to this country. Whether you've served in the military. All those things that show that you would be a desirable member of society. Because of the seriousness of the conviction, I have no discretion. I'm a delegate of the Attorney General. I have to follow the laws as written and the law—the way the Congress has written it, says that I can't even take those things into consideration. You're not eligible to apply for any of the applications that would allow me to consider those things."

The judge then issued his ruling: "It is HEREBY ORDERED that the respondent be removed from the United States."

On October 13, 2008, after he had exhausted his appeals, immigration authorities escorted him to a plane bound for the Dominican Republic. When he landed in Santo Domingo, police took him and other newly deported men and women to a police station for registration. A man took their photographs. Another man registered their fingerprints. They stood in different lines identified by the crimes that led to their deportation: drug felons here, possession of a firearm there, and so on. The intake took about two hours. The police taunted him. You're going down, motherfucker. Oh, we got another for drugs. We got you, motherfucker. Irizarry paid a cop $2,000 to delete his registration so when he looked for work, no potential employer would know he had been deported.

He found a job in Santiago, about two hours outside the capital, helping a man rent houses. When the work dried up, he returned to Santo Domingo. He works at call centers now, similar to telemarketing, and earns about $180 a month.

"Sometimes I think of going to Mexico and crossing over into the U.S.," Irizarry says. "If I could see my daughters. If I could see my father. He has Lou Gehrig's disease. I can't see him. Believe it or not, some people learn from their mistakes. I've learned. I would give what I don't have right now to see my family."

I want to call Feliz's mother, Juana, in Puerto Rico next, so Irizarry and I drive to his small apartment: bright yellow walls, tile floor, two bar stools the only furniture. He owns a Chihuahua, "Tony". The name reminds Irizarry of New York. Once we're inside, he double-locks the front door and I make the call to Puerto Rico.

Juana Feliz recalls how afraid she felt when Feliz deployed to Iraq. Many times he didn't call. She didn't know from day to day if he was alive or dead. She did not earn much so when he told her he had enlisted in the Army she thought, "Wow. He can have a bright future. The Army can do much more than I can do for him." She assumed the Army would enroll him in school. Instead, it sent him to war.

When he came home in 2005, he locked himself in his room. She didn't know what had happened over there. Something. Days, weeks, he didn't talk to her.

She did not hear about the fight over his Texas girlfriend until two months after it happened. You know how men are with their mothers, she says. Only when he was locked up did he tell her.

She does not understand why the United States wants to deport her son. She is suffering through what only a mother would understand and taking all kinds of medications for her nerves. She is sixty-one years old and fears for her health. Her son broke the law but she asks for forgiveness as a mother for her son.

"Please keep in mind it is not the end of the world," Irizarry tells her. "There are more people here like your son. You're not alone."

"You're in the Dominican Republic?"

"Yes. I'm a veteran. I was deported."

"Oh, my God, they did that to you, too?"

"Yes."

"I'm going to cry."

"Don't cry."

"I'll pray for you."

"Don't feel sorry for me. At least I'm not dead in Iraq. Neither is Feliz. You still have your son."

Later in the evening, Irizarry takes us to the house of a friend, Alberto Garcia. Garcia and Irizarry served together in Iraq. On December 14, 2000, New York City police arrested Garcia and charged him with conspiracy to sell drugs. He served seven years in prison. When he was released in August 2008, he was deported to his birthplace, the Dominican Republic.

"I was struggling economically, and I made a bad choice," he tells me, leading us out to a patio. "It was my first and only crime."

The patio could be the set of a play. Thick leafy plants enclose it. Pale yellow light from the interior of the house washes dully across the tiles. A black dog stands staring at us from a pen. We sit at a round glass table in thickly cushioned lawn chairs. Mosquitoes are merciless and Alberto's mother

sprays bug repellent. He and Irizarry sip beers. The humid
night air clings.

> Garcia: This guy you're writing about, Feliz, he don't know
> anything about this country. He'll need a lot of help.
> His family needs to take care of him. He has to be pa-
> tient. He needs to be put in place that's isolated so he
> can take it a little bit at a time. He will have to be re-
> born. I don't know.
>
> Irizarry: I think he should get a visa for Europe. Go. You
> don't have to come here. He'll have to learn Spanish
> even though he speaks it. Talk as they talk here or they'll
> know you're not from here. He has to listen, watch be-
> fore he opens his mouth. The Dominican Republic is
> like a jail. One big fucking yard on guard all the time.
> You haven't forgotten who you were and you have to
> become something different.
>
> Garcia: I think how things would have gone different for me
> if I'd joined the Army here. I tried. When I got out of high
> school in Santo Domingo, I was 16 but I had to wait until
> I was 18 to enlist. I thought, fuck this, and applied to go
> to the U.S. I had family in New York. When my green
> card application cleared, I left for New York and tried to
> enlist there but my English was no good. I got a job in a
> grocery store and then an electronics store. I worked, got
> my English together and joined the Army at twenty-five.
> Be All You Can Be. I thought it would be an opportunity
> to go to school, get a good job. March '97 to March '99.
> Honorable discharge. I had been to Kuwait and Iraq. I
> saw enough and got out. I swore on the flag for the U.S. I
> was willing to do it. I was lucky enough not to die.
>
> Irizarry: I was the first one in my family to join. Three
> cousins joined the Army because of me. Be All You Can
> Be, but just be a citizen. No one told me that.

Garcia: You got several things against you being deported. First, before you got deported you were incarcerated. When you get out everything is different.

Irizarry: People you knew think you're a bad person.

Garcia: They judge you. They don't visit you in prison. Then you come here. People say, where'd you learn English? The U.S. They know you're not from here. They know before you open your mouth. They know by how you walk. People know from that you're not from here.

Irizarry: I had to apply for a new ID card, new driver's license, everything.

Garcia: Me too. I didn't have any of that either. I'm lucky my mom is over here and I got two siblings so I got that support. My mother left to move to her place in New York, after I'd only been here for three months, I was all alone. Las Americas is the main street. I take it coming home from work. We're talking a fifteen- to twenty-minute walk. If you're working, get home before sunset, or be sure you have transportation to get you home. If you don't, eight out of ten times you'll be robbed on that stretch. You can rent a motorcycle for twenty-five pesos. Guys are on the street and they'll drive you to where you got to go. No problem. But if they see you walking alone one night and then they see you a second night, they'll watch you, get to know your schedule and rob you.

Irizarry: You learn to keep your mouth shut. Learn to lie. Look what happened with my military ID. It expired in '99. The police didn't bother to read it. And that's the police. It's shocking. Every time the police stop you, there's a good chance you're going in. They don't arrest you, but they take you in. The police stopped me with two other guys once. They had a record. I didn't know that at the time. I don't ask people, "Hey how many times have you been arrested?" Same way I don't tell people I'm deported, they don't say they've been arrested. Later on, I found out they'd been arrested for forgery. If you're with me and not doing anything wrong, you're fine. But the police recognized them. Pointed their fucking guns, automatic rifles. I thought they were going to kill us. I got my hands up in the air. Turn around, they said. I had nothing but my military ID. I'm a soldier for the U.S. They said, yeah, we'll find that out. You're with them, you're one of them. They took us in. We had to pay the cops to get some water. Ten pesos for a one-peso bottle of water. I couldn't call nobody. The police took one of the guys I was with and put a black bag over his head, plastic. Grabbed an onion, chopped it, and shoved it under the bag. When he breathed, he breathed onion, no air. They beat him on the back. A big stick on his legs, arms, and hands. They did that to both guys and kept asking about me. I met a guy in my cell that I recognized from my childhood. He was being held for robbery. He bribed his way out. I gave him my aunt's number. He called her when he got released. My aunt called a major in the station and I got out. I don't hang out with people now unless I know all about them. I keep to myself.

Garcia: I went to a job interview at a call center. I put down experience: TWA, U.S. Army, postal carrier, bus driver. They said, "Why are you applying for a job here?" I said, "OK, you know what, I'm not going to lie. I was incarcerated. I was deported." I still haven't gotten an answer from that company. I didn't know anyone. I didn't try to bribe. In my situation you have to bribe unless you clean your record like Hans. The job I got now, I knew a guy. He knows my family, knows my situation. I miss the American system. You pay taxes, you get some back. Pay Medicaid, you can walk into a hospital and be treated. If you have a reasonable paycheck you can get some goods with that money. You can grow as the country grows. I was a family guy. I took my kids out. Here I can't afford it unless I'm lucky and someone takes me out. I can't save $100 for sneakers. I can't send money for my daughters. Sometimes I think I'm doing good here. When I see my bills, not so good.

Irizarry: They still charge me for child support. My mom told me I just got a $26,000 bill.

Garcia: I wish I could go to the V.A. My knees are bad from jumping out of planes in the military.

Irizarry: My hearing is bad. You get nightmares?

Garcia: Sometimes. Get a beer or a shot of whisky. (Laughing) Once in Iraq I had an opportunity to drive into an oasis. We were in a Bradley tank. Me and Sergeant Cosco needed to take a dump.

Irizarry: He was a knucklehead.

Garcia: We found a place. A little oasis in the middle of the desert. Water. We hadn't showered in a month. (Turning serious) I had to drive the "Highway of Death." From Kuwait to Iraq. It was called the Highway of Death because there is a whole line of cars and trucks along it that got blown up.

Irizarry: I was in my Bradley a hair's breadth from a mine one time. A foot away. I called EOD (Explosive Ordnance Disposal) to remove it.

Garcia: Another thing I can't get over. I had to save a specialist from killing himself in a tent. Murray was the guy's name. I'm coming back from the latrine. Murray had an M-16 jammed down his throat. "I can't take it anymore," he said. I talked to him. Let him cry. "OK. You're not the only one who is afraid. You're not the

only one who has to step up." They sent him to the medic. I never saw him again.

Irizarry: He was a good guy. I remember him.

Garcia: "You're not the only one who is afraid, who has to
step up." I say those things to myself every day. I deal
with people, many of them on the street. My life is in
danger. I hold $1,000. I'm in a country that will kill you
for $10. I sell diesel. The bus drivers pay me, I have to
have change. I close at night in one of the most dangerous neighborhoods. I don't know. We used to be
working people in America. We got busted, and now
the whole universe is against us.

I leave the Dominican Republic the next morning and stop in
Miami to visit 65-year-old Guillermo Irizarry, Hans Irizarry's
father, at Franco Nursing and Rehabilitation Center. I want
to ask him about his son but his illness has progressed to
the point where he can no longer talk or move. He breathes
through a tube in his neck, is fed through another tube in
his stomach. The machines keeping him alive make clicking
noises. He lies on a bed, hands at his sides, palms down, and
stares at me. I don't want to leave without saying anything. I
approach his bed and introduce myself. I tell him I've seen
Hans. He has a job, I say. He has an apartment. He said to say
hello. He said he was sorry for messing up.

His father listens. Eyes tearing. Searching my face. He
opens his mouth, watching me, but makes no sound. I want
to think he heard and understood me. But there is no way to
know.

From Miami, I call Feliz and tell him about my trip to the
Dominican Republic. He asks about his wife. I tell him she is
doing well but worries about him.

Feliz tells me they have no need to worry. He knows he can adjust to the Dominican Republic if it comes to that. He has been to war and prison. He can do this, too. He has no interest in finding out whether he has post-traumatic stress disorder. He doesn't care. He is unwilling to fight as hard as his lawyer and his wife. He's almost done fighting. He's 31. He wants to do things other than fight. He wants it to be done.

Move to Survive

C esar Lopez admits he makes mistakes that could get him deported again. Stopped for speeding, fights. But the cops let him go. They had been Marines themselves. Leave no man behind. Once a Marine, always a Marine.

Stop fucking around, they told him. We'll let you go. But stay off the street.

He doesn't.

Deportation doesn't seem real to Lopez. The U.S. is his home. Has been since he was a little kid and his mother brought him to the States from Mexico. Like love, man. You can't help who you fall in love with. He can't help he grew up in America.

Lopez rises from a chair in his sister's Las Vegas house, where we'd met for the first time less than an hour ago.

"Let's eat," he says.

We pile into his white pickup, shoving folders and tools off the passenger side to make room for me. He tosses a Bible onto the dash.

"What're you hungry for?"

Before I can answer, he tells me he knows a place. Bonito Michoacan, a Mexican restaurant on South Decatur. He met his wife, Fabiola, there.

He works in a restaurant too, now. Lindo Michoacan, part of the Bonito Michoacan chain. Waits tables. A fucking U.S. Marine waiting tables. He's got plans. He might go to Tanzania. The Chinese and Europeans have invested there in solar energy. He used to install air conditioning and air circulation systems. He can do solar energy installation. Why not? But if he goes, there's no turning back.

At the Bonito Michoacan, Lopez orders more food than we can possibly eat. Chicken and steak tortillas, salad, refried beans, and brown rice. Live for today, man.

"You don't know what tomorrow will bring," he says, hunched forward, steadily tapping his feet, his dark eyes glinting with a nervous, gotta-roll energy. Plus, Lopez says, he's hungry. Hasn't eaten all day. Fuck it. Take out what we don't finish.

"Did I tell you about the kid?" he asks me.

"What kid?"

He tells me.

Lopez sits on a bus in Tijuana and looks out of a window at the towering, spiked fence separating Mexico and California. A kid with one arm squeezes into the seat beside him and watches him staring at the fence. He asks Lopez:

What are you doing?

Looking at the border, man.

Why?

I'm going to cross.

The bus stops and some elderly men and women with tanned, wizened faces pull themselves out of their seats, holding shopping bags and moving in a way that suggests their aged bodies contain greater burdens than their bags. Jostling forward, they step off the bus and release loud sighs. On the sidewalk, people mill about. They do not appear to be in any particular hurry, entering and leaving stores, their momentum influenced by the people around them. The men and women leaving the bus push through the throngs until they become part of the commotion. Lopez continues staring out of the window. He ignores the kid but is conscious of being watched by him. Lopez squints against the glare from the sunlight reflected off storefronts.

Really? How you going to do it? Cross, I mean?

I don't know.

Can I come with you?

With one arm? Lopez thinks. I don't think so.

No.

Because of this? The kid raises the stump of his left arm.

Yeah.

I'm not useless.

Lopez is a U.S. Marine. He was discharged from the Corps in 1995 as other than honorable for failure to adapt to the military. Translation: he didn't like people telling him what he could and could not do. The breaking point came when he requested leave to visit his fiancé. His company commander, Lt. Sweeney, who had had enough of Lopez and his in-your-face attitude, told him no. Lopez replied that he would see his fiancé with or without permission.

Why don't you just go, then? Lopez remembers Sweeney telling him. You're nothing but trouble. We don't want you here.

Lopez quit the Corps. Much later, the U.S. would decide it also did not want him. He was deported to Mexico in 2013, years after he had been arrested for transporting drugs in the 1990s and served time to pay for his mistake.

Lopez has no intention of living in exile. He has been re-conning the border for two weeks using what he learned in the Marine Corps to chart a route across the desert between Tijuana and San Diego and return home. Once a Marine, always a Marine. He doesn't care that the immigration judge told him he belonged in Mexico. He doesn't care that his birth certificate shows he was born in Juarez. He's not Mexican but American.

I'll show you, I'm not useless, the kid says.

Lopez looks at the boy, following shadows racing across his narrow face as the bus gathers speed and turns back into traffic. The kid looks right back at him.

OK, Lopez says.

Lopez gets off at the next stop and the boy follows him. Clothing stores with racks of shoes outside fill the sun-splayed sidewalk. Lopez doesn't want the kid tagging along while he recons another part of the border. He is an annoy-ing little shit, but Lopez can't help but like his moxie. He's pushy. He knows what he wants, doesn't waver, doesn't go with the flow, doesn't bullshit. Lopez appreciates that. He hates bullshitters.

Meet me there, the kid says and points at a taqueria.

Lopez maneuvers through the mobbed sidewalk, walking with a steady stride, sunglasses on, thin stubble lining his face, aware of his need to get physically fit after three months in the Houston Immigration Detention Center.

The fucking center charged for everything. Ramen noodles, ten for a dollar. He ate four crackers with peanut butter three times a day for protein. Oatmeal and fruit, too, when it was offered. The Marines taught him how to maintain his strength on little to no food. Even in the detention center, he was planning, charting his course back to his wife and their Las Vegas home.

Houston Immigration Detention Center, Houston, Texas
November 4, 2012
In here time stops, it does not count, the days, weeks, months lose their value. We lose our sense of self-worth. We forget what it is to be with our loved ones. I don't know how much longer they are going to keep me here.

But I know that there is only one thing for me to do when I am finally free. I will make my long journey back home through strange lands and unknown roads to Juarez. I will visit my godmother and then I am going to Tijuana where I plan on crossing over because I feel more comfortable in California. It is where I grew up and it seems like the perfect place to begin the second part of my journey back to regain my legal status. U.S. Marines don't give up. We adapt and overcome. Semper Fi.

I'm buying, the kid says walking up behind Lopez in the taqueria.

He slips off his shoulder pack and dumps candy onto the counter. Lopez stares at the small mountain of sweets.

You're not going to ask me where I got the money for this?

No. It's none of my business.

Did you see me go into those stores? I ask for a donation like I've got nothing. I don't ask for money. A donation. I get candy, toothpaste, cigarettes. Then I sell it. I do this all the time. I think it's time to do this in the United States.

Lopez laughs. They order beef tacos. The kid tells him his name: Juan. He lost his arm in a dirt bike crash. When they finish eating, the kid scoops his candy back into his pack. Lopez stands. He tells the kid he's leaving. Alone. The kid gives him his cell number.

Call me when you cross, the boy says.

A week later, Lopez leaves the kid a message. I'm going, he says, and tells him where to meet him. If you're not there, I'm gone.

He calls a friend in Las Vegas, Maria, a social worker he knew when he volunteered with homeless teens. While he was still reconning the border, he had offered her $1,000 to pick him up.

Are you ready? he asks her now. I'll be at the mountain tonight. Five miles out from Tecate.

Maria agrees. Lopez hangs up, writes down the date: March 14, 2013. He grabs his shoulder pack. He has one change of clothes, three bottles of water, and five chocolate-chip granola bars. His mother had given them to him when she visited a few days earlier. He did not tell her what he was planning. He wished she had not visited. She'd flown from her Las Vegas home to San Diego and then took a bus to Tijuana just to see him. The sad look in her eyes a week later as he walked her to the border to catch a flight back to the States depressed him and he had to fight back tears.

Of all my kids, the only one who is really an American is you, she told him. You have it in your blood. You're a Marine.

Lopez leaves the house where he has been staying with Marcos, a family friend. Marcos lives about five miles from the U.S. border.

See you later, Lopez tells him.

He catches a bus and arrives at three in the afternoon near where he intends to cross. He stares at the mountain he will climb. It rises above Tecate, Mexico, across from Tecate, California, an invisible man-made line separating the two towns. Maria would meet him on the U.S. side. Lopez looks for the kid but doesn't see him. He stops long enough to eat three beef tacos for a dollar.

Before he crosses, he shoots a video of himself with his cell phone. He has on sunglasses, t-shirt, and jeans. Head cocked to one side. I'm coming home, he says, one arm extended holding the phone. In case I die I want whoever sees this to know I love my family and the United States. As a Marine, I swore to give my life for my country. I can't live in Mexico like this. I'm an American.

Lopez reviews the video. He turns on the GPS app on his phone. He will send his family his location every half hour. Then he starts jogging toward the mountain, looking for ground sensors and trying to stay on hard surfaces so he doesn't set them off just as he had learned to do in the Marines to avoid stepping on land mines.

The kid calls him two hours later.

Oh, man, the kid says. I want to go with you.

Sorry. I'm already gone.

Fuck it. I've always wanted to go to Acapulco. I guess I'll go there.

OK.

Don't get caught.

I won't.

Lopez slips his phone back in his pocket and continues jogging. Too bad, kid. Just as well. Lopez would have dumped him anyway if he had to run from border patrol agents. Acapulco. Go for it, kid.

His phone rings again. Maria on the line.

I'm not going to make it, she says. My car broke down.

Houston Immigration Detention Center, Houston, Texas
November 2, 2012
*This is my true account of the events that have transpired to
propel me on this journey of redemption.*

*I am confined in a prison devoid of life, two rooms 60
feet by 50 feet on one side. The are 10 tables made of metal
with seats for 4, the metal tables anchored to the concrete
floor covered by a faded coat of gray paint that is scarred
by the desperate pleas of all the souls that came before me,
etched on the tables are the names of the men that society
has deemed undesirable or worthless and has locked away
to cover its shame.*

*The cinder block walls are painted white as if to con-
vince us prisoners of the purity and righteousness of our
confinement. And to make us believe in their mercy, they
provide us with two television sets bolted to opposite sides
of the room. One in English and one in Spanish. But I see it
for what it is, just another form of control to keep us docile
and subdued.*

*I always associated fire and brimstone with hell, I had
never imagined that hell on earth would be a cold prison
where the cold of this place is used as a weapon. A weapon
that dulls the senses that lashes you 24 hours a day, a cold-
ness that no matter how much you fight it, you will succumb
and it will force you into a fetal position to allow your body
a small degree of warmth and comfort.*

He was five, maybe younger, he doesn't remember, when
his mother brought him to southern California after his
father left her. Left her with him and three other siblings in
Juarez. She fell into a depression. Her uncle in LA told her to

come to California. She took Lopez and his sister on a bus
from Juarez to Chihuahua. From there they caught a plane
to Tijuana, where his mother's in-laws watched him while
she crossed into California on foot. Before she left, she told
Lopez he would be with her soon. It took her two days to
reach her uncle's house in LA.

Lopez waited. He has a hazy memory of that time. The
house in Tijuana stood near a cliff. His mother's in-laws had
children of their own and he remembers being quite happy
playing with them. His mother sent for him on the Fourth of
July. A member of the family—he doesn't remember who—
gave him NyQuil so he would sleep when they drove him
across the border. They also had purchased a fake passport
for him. He remembers seeing fireworks all the way into
LA through groggy, half closed eyes. He remembers feeling
sleepy but happy.

His mother met him at Echo Park. She hugged and
kissed him. He laughed. From then on Mexico became a
memory. He returned with his mother only to visit family.
LA was home now. He grew up without supervision, his
mother always working. Cashier, waitress, seamstress, any
kind of work she could find. Friends of his mother watched
over him when she worked. He says he was "community
raised."

In LA, he could hop on a bus and be anywhere in minutes. He'd skip school and catch a ride to Venice Beach.
Roam around, jump in the water. He'd then wander off to
Griffith Park and hike around the hills. He remembers a
movie theater on Sunset Boulevard. One dollar, two movies. Ragged-ass place. He'd see rats fighting on the floor. He
watched black-and-white war movies and became enthralled
with the notion of giving his life for a greater good. A heroic
death, moving last words. His name remembered. He would

be the hero who protected old people, and children who had no one else to watch over them.

The real world was different. White boys at school didn't allow him to hang out with them because he was a Mexican. The Mexicans didn't like him either. He was into computers, not cars like they were. When he visited his mother's family in Juarez, the Mexicans there gave him shit for living in the U.S.

He never did the gang thing. His mother told him, "I came here to work. Don't shame me and become a gang member." He used to get beat up all the time but he never joined. In the ninth grade he got shit-kicked real bad. His mother wept. "I'm sorry I can't give you a better life," she said. Lopez stayed at home after that, his "cave" he called it. When he went out, he didn't hang around. Got to where he was going and came home. Otherwise, it was get your ass kicked from Point A to Point B. He didn't have to see anyone to feel the need to bolt back to his house. When he did see someone, he made calculations. What's he up to? What does he want with me? Is he going to jiujitsu my ass? Later, in the Marines, he learned to fight back.

He got his green card when he was 17 and found a job washing dishes in Beverly Hills. Nibblers Restaurant. Wilshire Boulevard. His uncle got him the job. The owner was cool. Paid a good wage, six, seven bucks an hour. But he knew the job would lead nowhere.

When he turned 18 and was a senior in high school, Lopez's mother told him she was moving to Las Vegas. She was tired of California, didn't like the constant, small earthquakes that rattled her house.

I did all I could do for you, she told him. You have to find your own way now.

He stayed in LA and applied to Oregon State, UCLA, and the University of Texas, El Paso. He told his mother he would buy her a Cadillac when he made his first million. Oregon

State and the University of Texas accepted him but his mother didn't have money for school. That first million would have to wait.

In 1993, with no other options, he decided to join the military. He took a bus to a recruiting station near the Capitol Records building. He walked into a large open room. Recruiters representing the five branches of the military—Air Force, Army, Coast Guard, Marine Corps, and Navy—lingered by their desks. Each recruiter told him to sign up with them. We're the best, they said. Then one guy came out of a back room. Shut the fuck up, he said to the recruiters. Sit right over there, son. He pointed to a table with a sign. "U.S. Marine Corps." The other recruiters said nothing. They were enlisted men. The Marine was an officer. Lopez showed him his green card.

You're fine, the officer told him. You'll get your citizenship in boot camp.

Lopez didn't care. He already thought he was an American. Hell, he came up in LA, man.

He enlisted in the Marines.

After Maria tells Lopez she cannot pick him up, he calls Fabiola.

Maria backed out, he says. I'm moving forward. I can't go back.

Fabiola tells him, You don't need to come back. I'll go to Mexico. I'll get a job there.

No, Lopez said. I'm not giving up.

Fabiola says nothing. When Lopez insists on doing something, there's nothing she can say to stop him. He had told her before he even reached Tijuana that he would cross. I'll plan a route and get in shape for a week, he said. Two weeks later, he called her at 5 a.m.

Today's the day, he said.

Oh, my God, Fabiola said.

Lopez gets off the phone with his wife and calls his sister Raquel. He tells her what he told Fabiola and hangs up. He needs to conserve the cell phone battery for the GPS. Raquel calls Fabiola.

You got to stop him, Raquel says. You're the only one he listens to. What if something happens to him?

No, Fabiola says. He won't listen to me. He'll do it.

Raquel thinks her brother has lost his mind. He's crazy, she tells her husband. He risks his life for what? Then her mother calls to ask if she has heard from Lopez. Marcos, the family friend, had called her to say Lopez was crossing tonight.

Is he planning to come back? Lopez's mother asks Raquel.

I don't know, Raquel said. She doesn't like lying to her mother, but she doesn't want to tell her Lopez is stuck in the desert without a ride. Her crazy little brother. She was so proud of him when he joined the Marines. He looked so handsome in his uniform. She told him when he was deported, We'll send you money to help you settle.

You know how much money I'd need? Lopez had said. I'm coming back.

You could be put in jail again, Raquel told him.

Yeah.

You could die.

Yeah.

Lopez.

We'll see what happens, he said.

Lopez's mother gets off the phone with Raquel. She knows he's crossing. Something in Raquel's voice told her. When Lopez had been detained in Houston, his mother had hoped he would not be deported. After he was, she called her family in Juarez so he would have a place to stay. She wept. She had struggled to make a living in the U.S. for herself and her children. Lopez didn't know anyone in Mexico. Still, she felt confident he would make it wherever he went. He was stubborn that way.

She considered moving to Mexico and living with him. When she saw him in Tijuana, she had watched him taking note of the border. He was quiet. She knew he was plotting something.

What do you think he's going to do? Marcos had asked her. Cross?

Yes, his mother said. He has that look in his eye.

She worried about him. He picked fights with U.S. border agents, shouting at them, taking videos. Come on, shoot me, he'd scream. She told him to calm down but he wouldn't listen.

When it was time for her to return to Las Vegas, Lopez walked her to the border.

See you soon, he had said.

Houston Immigration Detention Center, Houston, Texas
November 3, 2012
Another day spent with the burden of the past, I wake up and thank God for another day, for giving me clarity of mind, and hope in my heart. I like to believe that the Lord has a plan for me, the problems of my youth are long gone, that anger and fear that marked my early life are now just a distant reminder of how much I had strayed from God, and I believe that happened 'cause I never really had a strong understanding of the meaning of God and the salvation that comes with this belief.

There are 40 men total, including myself in this holding cell. 40 men from all over the world, every one of them has their own story to tell, but most won't. I sense a common feeling of indifference, and even a sense of joy at being imprisoned, for

*in reality if you are in here and you can withstand being de-
prived of your liberty, the system will provide all your basic
needs. In here you don't have to worry about shelter or paying
rent; In here you don't have to worry about food, 3 basic meals
are provided, even if it's food I wouldn't feed a homeless man,
but it's enough to provide sustenance for the body.*

*This morning we were fed a half pint of milk with a
handful of corn flakes, 3 small pancakes about 3" in diam-
eter with one slice of bologna, two packets of sugar. The system also provides access to basic hygiene, a place to shower
and small toilets. We are also allowed one hour of outside
recreation. When you add up all of these factors, it's easy to
understand why a great number of inmates begin to enjoy
their bonds. As for me, I will never, ever submit.*

Lopez did his basic at Fort Lee, Virginia. One morning, as
he was mopping the floor of the barracks, a sergeant told
him, That's not how you swab! Start all over. The sergeant
came back an hour later. I said, that's not how you do it! He
punched Lopez, knocked him out cold. Woke up in the infir-
mary. Eighth week in boot camp. A doctor asked him what
happened. He said nothing. He was a Marine now.

He weighed 155 pounds when he enlisted. Skinny little shit. But after 13 weeks of boot camp he had put on 30
pounds. The Corps wired him to kill. What makes the grass
grow? Blood! Blood! Blood!

But he had no place to release the furious energy that
came with all this new wiring. He never went to war. Never
experienced that sense of danger, adventure, weaponry. He
would always regret that. That blaze of glory. That amped-up
feeling to kick ass. You can't just put the genie back in the
bottle after you're wired to kill. Like having blue balls. After
all the drills, Blood! Blood! Blood! All the arousal. Maybe
it was a good thing he didn't go to war. He has an explosive

temper to this day. Imagine what he'd be like if he'd seen battle.

After boot camp, he was stationed in San Diego. He had wanted to be an aviation mechanic but instead trained to be a bulk fuel specialist and pumped gas for two months. Then he was sent to Oceanside for guard duty. Thirty-day rotations. Thirty days guarding the motor pool, 30 days guarding the Army barracks, 30 days guarding the kitchen, 30 days guarding the San Diego/Tijuana border.

One time, as the sergeant of the guard watched him patrolling the border, Lopez stopped a young Mexican couple, a couple with kids.

You're trespassing on military property. You will be fired upon if you don't stop, he shouted at them.

We got lost, the husband said. The coyote left us.

Get out of here, Lopez told them.

He pointed.

Go that way. There's a bus stop. You'll be there in an hour. The bus'll take you to Anaheim. Do you have money?

The coyote took it.

Lopez gave them 20 bucks. When he returned to base at the end of his 12-hour shift, the sergeant stopped him.

What would you say if someone said they saw you with some people?

They were just kids on the beach.

Say if I were to tell you I watched with night goggles?

Well, we'll have a different conversation then.

I saw you let a couple go. Why?

I can't do that. My mother came into this country that way. I did, too. I can't do that.

Fucking Lopez. Get the fuck out of my sight.

He barely slept that night. He thought he was in deep shit. In the morning, he got up, ate, stayed worried. Other soldiers in the mess hall whispered to him: We heard what you did.

Oh, shit, he thought.

The sergeant called him to his office an hour later.

You're confined to your quarters. Turn in your weapon. You don't move, don't shit, until I tell you.

He was busted down to provide security for E Club, the enlisted club. A fucking bar. He carried a nightstick for a weapon, nothing more. He broke up a few fights between drunken, pimply young Marines. Got in a few, too, but he never threw the first punch.

Most of the scraps he got into came from sounding off on people who got in his face. He was angry at the world. Blood! Blood! Blood! But it was more than that. Or maybe all that screaming for blood got him thinking of his own blood. Of family. Of his absent father. His old man bought him new underwear one time. That's his only memory of doing something with his father. New underwear. Plastic wrapped. Fruit of the Loom or some shit. As a kid, when he'd visit family in Juarez, he spent a lot of time looking for his father in cantinas. He'd find him kissing waitresses. The old man'd say, How's my boy? Here. Here's five bucks.

Lopez wanted his father to kiss him, too, love him, too. He didn't want his money but he took it. He took what he could get.

When his father got sick, was dying, Lopez's godfather said, You need to see him. Lopez thought, Fuck him, he can die. His godfather got mad. He wants to see you, he said. Ain't that nice, Lopez said. What about all the time I wanted to see him? How's that?

In the desert between Mexico and Tecate, California, Lopez weighs his options. He does not have enough food or water to make it on foot. But he is on foot. What is he looking at, two, three days? What do you do, Marine? He will stretch what food he has by eating two granola bars every three hours. They won't last but he knows that in mountain valleys he will find water and food. He learned that in boot camp. Look for creeks. Eat vegetation. Dandelion leaves. What else? Beans. Bugs.

He picks the most treacherous terrain to make it difficult for border agents to follow him. The water he finds tastes cool and piney. He spends his first night on the edge of a cliff beneath a rock ledge. Stars interrupt the black sky above him. He awakens to hear a border agent talking to another agent standing on the ledge above him.

That fucker still here? one agent says.

He's gotta be, the other agent said. Someone tripped the sensor.

They talk about going into the valley below, the same route Lopez plans to walk. He adjusts his plans. As soon as the agents leave, he hikes back up the mountain he just descended hours before. He traverses four mountains before he stops again, his first night out. Middle of the desert. Fucking cold. He lies in the dark, staring into the night. He hears a ping on his GPS. Then his phone dies.

Houston Immigration Detention Center, Houston, Texas
December 9, 2012
One of the blessings of my situation is that it has brought my family closer once again. That is not the case for Elizandro one of my cell mates. Elizandro is a native of El Salvador, he had been in the U.S. previously for two years and decided to go visit his family in El Salvador. Upon his return, he was apprehended and deportment procedures started. His family got him a lawyer to help him claim asylum, he also got a bond set for $5000.00 which his father sent to his brother in New Jersey so he could pay his bond. Unfortunately for Elizandro his brother so far has refused to pay the bond and

looks like he is going to be stuck in here for a while longer. Even sadder is that he helped his brother come to The United States by paying his coyote's fee and giving him shelter when he arrived.

I wonder what kind of person you have to be to do this kind of despicable act to your own brother. Poor guy. A week ago he was excited and happy because he was going home. He started to give away the little food that he had left. Now he is visibly depressed and just wondering when and if he is ever going to get out.

Even though I am just as depressed as everyone in here, I sit and wait, I talk to my wife more often again but with more moderation due to the astronomical cost of the calling cards they sell here, and I talk to my sister and my mom at least once a week. It's hard for me to wait in here, knowing that the sands of my life clock slowly fill the bottom of the hour glass and I will never get this time back, I think of the decisions I have made in my life that have brought me to this point, and I think I am ready to tell the story of the events in 2000 near Tucumcari New Mexico, that is the second charge the government has against me, but I will write that tomorrow because this is what hurts me more than the 1995 Kansas case and I want to reflect on that period of my life to accurately and to the best of my ability describe this period of my life.

Looking back, he would describe the Corps as one of the greatest adventures of his life. He loved the way they screamed at you. Jump out of the bus, bitches, five seconds. He loved that because he found it so funny. The contorted faces, the bulging eyes. The absurdity. Why did they get so worked up for some dumb shit like getting off a bus? He laughed at the stupid stuff.

He had problems following orders for the sake of following orders because some guy in a uniform told him to do
some fucking thing. He needed a reason. The mindlessness
of the orders tested his humor. Like one time, he had to hike
10 miles in the mountains outside San Diego where he was
stationed after boot camp. Return to base and out again,
back and forth, back and forth, 10 miles each way all day, all
night. He was right up there, never fell behind. But he told
the commanding officer he thought it was stupid. If he was
late for morning roll call, the CO would write him up. Shoes
weren't tied, wrote him up. Uniform askew, wrote him up.
Well, fuck, he just kept mouthing off. He loved the Corps for
the same reason he hated it. The stupid stuff. It made him
laugh, it drove him bat shit.

Lopez, you need to settle down, the CO told him. Enjoy
the view. You can tell your grandkids about it.

He was 19. He had not learned to keep his opinions to
himself. He never would. While he was still enlisted, he met
a woman in Juarez while he was visiting family. They got
married, had two daughters. But he and his fellow Marines
in San Diego liked to mess around with a lot of girls. His
wife caught him cheating in Tijuana. She told the commander what happened. Said Lopez beat her up, too. He said he
didn't. No charges were filed.

In 1995, after serving in the Marines just two years, Lopez
received an other than honorable discharge. Failure to adapt
to the military. The complaints his wife had made against
him hadn't helped.

After his discharge, the couple tried to make their marriage work. He didn't want his kids to grow up without a
father. He didn't want them looking for him in cantinas.

They moved to El Paso to be near family in Juarez. In a
Juarez bar one night a bartender hit on Lopez. Her boyfriend
approached holding a pistol. The bartender, he said, was

his girl. Young stud that he was, Lopez didn't give two shits about that.

Apparently, she don't like you that much, Lopez said.

The boyfriend raised his gun but a friend stopped him.

Why'd you say that? the bartender asked Lopez.

I ain't scared. It's a public place.

The boyfriend left, waited outside for Lopez and introduced himself. Nazario.

I'm impressed, Nazario said. You don't scare. I'm looking for people like you. I sell pot in Illinois, Florida, Texas, Colorado. I'll pay you $100 for every pound you carry. You in?

In, Lopez said.

He hauled dope twice a month and sometimes earned as much as $20,000. He thought it was fucking awesome, a real high, no shit. Knowing the risks. Knowing that everyone he passed on the Interstate had no idea what he held in his trailer. And the money knocked him out. He hadn't been to war but maybe, he thought, this was like war. Undercover. Behind enemy lines. If you're caught, you're fucked. Whatever it was, he loved it. A fucking rush. His own boss, too. No one bothered him. He had a schedule. Nazario gave him a truck and told him where to go.

I'll get it there, Lopez would say.

Sometimes, he carried the weed to a Juarez warehouse for distribution later, or to a "drop house" in El Paso. He liked to think he had scruples. He wouldn't deliver drugs, chemicals. Marijuana was different. If it's green, it's natural. God put it on earth. What's the harm?

The job didn't last long. In October 1995, on his fifth haul, his rig broke down on I-70 near Watson, Kansas. The radiator overheated and blew. A double compartment on the floor near the chassis held 250 pounds of pot. He grabbed his backpack and got out of the truck. He wasn't sticking

A deported veteran stands at the wall between Tijuana and San Diego with a banner protesting the removal of veterans to Mexico

Hector Barajas-Varela irons his Army uniform as he prepares to attend a protest against the deportation of veterans

Deported Army veteran Alfredo "Al" Varon Guzman sitting on his cot in the Bunker

Iraq War Army veteran Neuris Feliz in his Lancaster, PA apartment.

Olivia Segura visiting the grave of her Army veteran daughter, Ashley

Hector Barajas-Varela at his desk in the Bunker

Deported Army vet Oscar Leyva in the front room of the Bunker

Deported Marine Cesar Lopez holding a certificate from the Marines

around with a vehicle filled with a couple hundred pounds of weed. He had had a bad feeling about the vehicle but didn't take the time to check it out. Greed, man, it clouded his reasoning. He started walking when the highway patrol showed up.

I'm going to get a tow, Lopez said.

I'll call one for you, the officer said.

She made a call. Then she let a German shepherd out of her squad car and walked it around the truck. The dog didn't seem to sniff out anything. But its tail sure was wagging.

Permission to search your car, sir, the officer said.

No.

Are you carrying drugs?

I'm not saying I am.

The officer looked around the outside of the van.

You're up to something, she said.

We all are, he said.

The officer got down on her knees and looked under the truck. She noticed the gas tank. It had been cut to make space for the drugs. The tank, she said. Looks modified. She made another call. Forty minutes later, she got a court order to search the van. She found the drugs.

Looks like this trip won't pay out for you, she told Lopez.

Yeah, it won't this time.

He pled guilty, throwing himself on the mercy of the court. He couldn't think of anything else to do. Hard to deny what had been found in his truck.

I couldn't find a job, he told the judge. I was approached to make money hauling pot and I took it.

Young man, the judge said. I don't know what to make of you. I'm going to bet on you being in the wrong place at the wrong time. I'm giving you five years' probation. Go home and be a father to your kids.

Lopez wakes up starving his second day in the desert. Still dark. He is out of granola bars, and eating vegetation doesn't cut it. He aches from sleeping on the hard ground, what little sleep he has. He looks up at the stars and stretches, body grimed with dirt and sweat. Well, it's better than being locked up. In the detention center, eighty other men along with Lopez faced deportation. Six of them had been in the U.S. all their lives. Some couldn't even speak Spanish.

Whoever controlled the thermostat kept it cold as shit. The saddest thing he saw? One blind, old man in chains. Sixty-something years old. Chained, man, at the wrists, waist and legs, and he can't see. Where was he going to go?

Some pods held eighty people, other pods forty to fifty people. Some of them belonged to cartels. Lopez sat down to eat one afternoon and a cartel guy said, that's my spot. Two guys stood behind him.

I didn't see your name, Lopez told him. You're welcome to come take it.

He slept with one eye open after that.

Chicken. Chicken was the only real food they served. Chicken made for a good day. One time when chicken was served, the supervisor miscounted the number of trays that needed to be distributed. The detainees told him he was off by one person. No, I counted, the supervisor said. That means someone will go without food, Lopez told him. Un plato mas, por favor. No, the supervisor said again, I counted. He accused the detainees of hiding a tray so that they could get extra food. Lopez asked to speak to the commanding officer. The CO ordered the guards to look for the tray they said was hidden. They didn't find it. Still they refused to serve the additional meal. Lopez chose to be the one not to eat. What the hell? He had a stash of crackers and peanut butter.

He shakes his head, looks around the flat desert landscape. He asks God for guidance, keeps moving. Movement is life, he learned in the Marines. You move to live. He runs for twenty minutes and stops, listens. When the sun comes fully up, he studies the rocky terrain before him. He looks for border patrol vehicles in the distance, sees one and watches it start and stop, start and stop. He times it. Ten minutes from point A to B. He calculates what the response time would be should the agent see him. Ten, fifteen minutes, maybe. Usually when they stop it means they've caught someone. They'd be a while. He'd have time to book. Another man's bad luck, his good fortune.

He continues watching. The border patrol agent stays put. Maybe he's nabbed someone. Time to roll, Lopez says to himself. He runs down a mountain toward a cliff, slips, falls, and starts sliding. He flails, tries to hold onto something, anything before he drops off the cliff. He digs his fingers into the rocky ground, grabs some scrub brush. It holds him. He hears a rock fall. Six seconds later it hits the ground. Terminal velocity of a falling rock is 110 miles an hour. Had he been that rock, that would have hurt. He thanks God for the plants. He hauls himself into a sitting position. He remains still, tries to pretend he is on a camping trip to get the fear out of him.

When he calms down, he starts moving again. The border patrol vehicle revs up and turns in his direction. Two spotlights gleam, illuminating the night, entrapping bats in the glare. White and blue lights. Opening up the whole canyon. A blue light falls across Lopez. He hears frantic beeping and drops to the ground. This is it. Busted. The vehicle flies by him, skids to a stop. What's going on? Lopez wonders. Has he nailed someone? He doesn't know. He crawls under an embankment and sinks between the roots of a tree. The border patrol agent stands about 50 feet away. The wide range of his lights fall across Lopez. Does he see him? What should he do? Shit. He counts. Five, ten seconds. Long time. Then he hears the vehicle leave, the noise of its engine and the crunch of rocky ground beneath its tires moving farther and farther away. Lopez gives a thumbsup to the stars.

Houston Immigration Detention Center, Houston, Texas
January 4, 2013

It has been a few days since I last imprinted my thought on paper. The reason is that I have been overwhelmed by the agonizing specter of confinement. I have been paralyzed by fear and impotence. I am losing the battle to this torture, I can feel how this intangible juggernaut tramples over me, slowly. Every day that goes by I can feel how its tentacles squeeze the strength, life, and will out of mental defenses. One by one my abilities and fortifications are being destroyed. Like an advanced fail-safe mechanism, red lights are being activated, signalizing the total collapse of the system.

Anxiety is the first specter to torment me, haunting me with visions of a bleak future; a future of defeat and wasted time, a place where after enduring a prolonged stay behind bars, the loss of all of our savings, our business, and most of our material possessions, I end up being deported to the country of my birth, a place so alien to me that just to think about the possibility brings a cold chill to my spine and makes the hair on my whole body stand up. Uncertainty erodes my sanity, I have started to lose track of time, day from night, time of the day. I can't sleep, I lay awake while everyone else is sound asleep, my mind has started to unbalance itself again. Anger builds inside of me like a dormant volcano, I want to lash out and vent all of my built-up fury at the world, but I can't, this monster that tortures me is a mythical Hydra, even if I could lash out and cut off one of its heads, in this case be it the guards, prosecutor, the judge or any of its representatives, it would be fruitless, more problems would rise up to compound my suffering.

My only choice is to endure and pray that time disappears faster than my hopes and dreams. Despair surrounds me, like ravenous hyenas circling a wounded, wild beast, I sense it, I can hear it laughing at me, taunting me, intimidating me, waiting me out. I am lashing out at my wife, I can't contain myself, every time she tells me that she is suffering just like me, I get mad, I don't doubt that she is hurting, but to say that her suffering is the same as mine, upsets me. Liberty is one of God's greatest gifts to man, and men have taken my freedom away. For crimes that I committed in my youth. Crimes for which I have already paid back to society in spades. The poor choices I made then have followed me long after I fulfilled my sentence.

Lopez returned to El Paso after the Kansas judge let him off. He vowed to himself to stay straight. He worked a legit job making Mr. Potato Head molds. He enrolled in Western Technical College. He was turning his life around but not completely. Mr. Potato Head didn't pay as well as hauling dope, and Lopez and his wife bumped heads over money. They divorced in 1999 and shared custody of their daughters.

Divorce added to his financial problems. Child support, rent, it adds up. He was in trouble with money again. Friends told the Juarez drug dealer, Nazario, that Lopez was back in town. Nazario offered him work. Same thing, hauling pot. He took it to finish school. Then, he swore to himself he'd be done. He carried 30 to 50 pounds. Las Cruces, Amarillo, within the area.

He graduated in 2000 with an associate degree in computer science and quit transporting pot. Got a job at Intel

Corporation and made a lot of money. Then in 2012, Rudy, his best friend in college, got in a jam, falling behind on his student loans.

I need you, Rudy told him. Help me out with your dope connections.

No, Lopez said.

Rudy was too submissive and nervous to get into the drug game, a little white dude who freaked out about everything. A parking ticket. And you would think that he had been charged with armed robbery. But he was a persistent little prick. Lopez finally agreed to introduce him to his contacts and no more. Nazario hired Rudy to transport forty pounds of marijuana.

Come with me, he asked Lopez.

Lopez was like, Shit, all right. I'll do it this once. Just to help him out. Shouldn't have. Should have kept saying no. The highway patrol nailed them speeding on I-40 west to Amarillo. One hour away from the drop house. Snowing, cold. Rudy shaking.

You look nervous, the cop said.

The cop got a search warrant for the car. Lopez took the rap. Rudy had no priors. He was crying and they hadn't even been booked yet. He wouldn't make it in jail. One more felony won't hurt me, Lopez thought.

Funny thing is, he didn't do a day in jail. He cooperated with the DA and informed on the dealer. In return, he received a one-year deferred sentence. He moved to Las Vegas to be with his mother and sister. Texas was just trouble. He never heard from Rudy again.

From 2003 to 2005, he worked construction. He'd show up at job sites and the foreman would ask, what do you know how to do? Forklift, throw bricks, carry, Lopez said. He worked from site to site. From Las Vegas to New Mexico to Colorado to Wyoming to California to Arizona to Las Vegas again.

But he got tired of the traveling. Back in Las Vegas, he took a course installing air conditioning units. He volunteered with Help of Southern Nevada, a social service agency, after a cop ticketed him for speeding and he was sentenced to 120 hours of community service. He worked with inner city kids, encouraging them not to make the same mistakes he had with drugs. In 2011, he saw Fabiola for the first time in Bonito Michoacan restaurant. She was a hostess. Her black hair hung down to her shoulders, and she had a tight-ass figure. Her smile made his tongue stumble. When she brought his order, he complained about the food. You got this wrong. She had gotten nothing wrong. He just said that to talk to her. To prevent her from leaving his table. They married a year later in 2012.

One day, a work supervisor told him about a Costa Rican company that needed guys to install AC in a new hotel. Four G's a month. Lopez went for it. The job lasted four months. On October 28, 2012, Lopez returned to Las Vegas with a layover in Houston. He sent a text to Fabiola that he was back in the States.

When Fabiola got off work that afternoon, she had not heard from Lopez. She sent him a text. He responded, Oh, well, they got me here. Checking on something. Everything is fine.

But everything was not fine. When customs agents had run his passport through the computer, his felony record came up. They also saw he was not a citizen. Lopez knew nothing about the immigration law that permitted the deportation of non-citizens convicted of criminal offenses, but the customs agents did. He was detained and sent to the Houston Detention Center.

I'm going to stay here, he texted Fabiola at 7 p.m. I'm here for the felony.

You already paid for it, she wrote back.

Yeah, everything is going to be OK.

At 9:30, he sent his last text: They're taking my phone. Can't call you. Just wait. I'm not getting out.

Lopez's family hired a lawyer and shelled out $7,000 but got nowhere. At an immigration court hearing on January 6, 2013, a judge told Lopez he was not an American.

I'm sending you home.

Los Angeles? Lopez asked.

What?

LA is home.

No, you're going to Mexico.

I guess I'll be back, Lopez said.

His lawyer said if he could shell out an additional $25,000 he could file an appeal, but the family didn't have any more money.

What do you want us to do? Fabiola asked her husband.

Don't spend any more money.

But you're going to Mexico. You don't know anyone there.

No, Lopez said again.

On January 17, 2013, Lopez wrote in his diary:

I have decided not to appeal the deportation order, and once again I will venture into the U.S. as an illegal alien. It's weird to be back at this point in my life, but I am an American whether they like it or not. Just because a judge said that I am not an American, it does not mean that I am going to stop liking football, stop enjoying my way of life as an American, and most importantly, that won't stop me from believing in America. That it's a land of justice. Where right will overcome wrong. I believe I have been wronged by lawyers and unjust judges and I will continue to fight until those wrongs are righted.

I will continue to relate my journey until it comes to an end. Looks like the next part of my journey is going to take me from the border town of Laredo in Mexico to Mexicali or San Diego where I plan on trying to cross the border again into my country illegally for the first time in twenty years. I have to speak to my wife and decide what we are going to do as a couple, I want to try to cross at least one time, but I don't know what she might think if the risks out weigh the benefits. Only God knows, and I hope we make the right decisions. May God bless me on my journey.

Five weeks later, on February 25, 2013, the anniversary of his marriage to Fabiola, a shackled Lopez walked onto a bus bound for Laredo. He had his two bags of luggage from Costa Rica, money, a credit card, and his Nevada ID.

I'm sorry you're being deported, a guard told him. I know you're a Marine.

I'm sure the guy who killed Jesus apologized, too, Lopez said.

One deportee on the bus wore a Captain America T-shirt.

Hey, they're deporting Captain America! Lopez said.

You better shut your mouth, the driver said. You dirty Mexicans, settle the fuck down.

What are you going to do? Deport me? Lopez said.

Three other deportees wore only paper hospital gowns. Dogs with a canine unit had torn up their clothes when they were detained. Lopez gave them some of his shirts and pants. Karma, baby. What the hell, it made his bags lighter.

At Laredo, guards told the deportees to walk across the bridge into Laredo, Mexico. An ICE agent hugged Lopez.

Good luck, Marine, he said.

Lopez hated Laredo. Mexican military all over the place. He heard gunshots every three or four hours. He caught a bus to Juarez. The bus stopped three times at checkpoints. Everybody got off. Lopez was taken off and strip-searched. They went through his wallet, examined his Nevada driver's license.

You don't belong here.

I know, Lopez said. You're preaching to the choir, man. I know.

In Juarez, he met his daughters, who still lived in El Paso with their mother.

I'm crossing back, he said.

His youngest daughter offered to drive him out. He told her no. He didn't want to put her at any risk.

He stayed at his godmother's house in Juarez. She took him to movies and drove him around town. Alone, he looked inside cantinas, chasing the ghost of his father.

After three days in Juarez, he took a bus to Tijuana. The city was familiar terrain. He had patrolled the border as a Marine. He got on Craigslist to find a coyote. I am an American looking for travel agent to return to the U.S., he posted. A couple of people contacted him but wanted $15,000. A lot of money, a lot of risk, and no guarantee of success. He decided to cross on his own.

The next day, he caught a bus for Playas de Tijuana, a borough surrounded by the Pacific Ocean on one side and the U.S. on the other. The wall separating Mexico and the U.S. ran into the ocean. Lopez followed the wall east toward the town of Tecate near Tijuana and across the border from Tecate, California. Hard asses working for human trafficking cartels and who Lopez thought would kill mother fuckers as soon as look at them sat at various points along the wall charging migrants to cross. Lopez told them nothing. Just scoping it out, he'd say. He didn't want to offend them, didn't want to ask them questions. When it came to the cartels, he didn't know Peter from Paul. He didn't want to get in trouble with Peter and find out he had also offended Paul.

He moved further down the wall away from the cartel guys. Through the bars of the wall, he took his time observing American immigration officers lecturing recruits about the border. The recruits asked questions. Lopez had his own questions, especially about fog. He remembered how fog rolled into LA. To cross, he needed fog for concealment.

What do you do when there's fog? a recruit asked as if he had read Lopez's mind.

Double patrols and put on infrared, an officer told him.

Lopez spent his days walking every inch of the border wall from Playas de Tijuana to Tecate and back again. He found a stretch near Tecate where the wall went up the side of a mountain just so high until it ended. On the other side of it, the U.S. border.

Here, Lopez told himself, I'll cross here.

He visited that spot every day, going at different times to get a sense of the border patrols in the area.

He looked for drones, listened for the hum they made. He didn't know if the U.S. used drones along the border but he guessed they did. He watched how agents used infrared lighting and assumed he would need a route where he could hide under rocks the infrared could not penetrate. He studied Google Earth maps. He observed the shift changes of border patrols. Every twelve hours, he wrote in his notebook.

Some days, he ran to the mountain and crossed a few feet to the U.S. side, assuming that he would step on ground sensors. Then he would haul ass and hide in bushes back on the Mexican side, timing the response of the border agents. Twenty minutes. He'd have twenty minutes to run until he'd have to stop and hide.

He tested his theory day after day, making trial runs to the mountain and back to Mexico again within twenty minutes. One afternoon, some border agents spotted him.

Amigo, amigo, one of the agents said, placing a hand on his gun.

Hey, I'm unarmed, Lopez said.

What are you doing? You're in America.

No, this is Mexico.

Are you trying to cross?

No, Lopez said.

I see you.

I'm on the Mexican side, Lopez said.

What are you doing?

I'm looking for Aztec gold.

How do you know English?

I'm a Marine.

Just know we're going to catch you. We catch everybody.

Lopez watched them leave. The weather forecast called for fog. Time to roll. He'd like a few more days observing the border. Fuck it. He could only prepare so much.

Houston Immigration Detention Center, Houston, Texas
January 16, 2013
This place is a mad house. I have been behind bars for almost three months, and I have been housed in three different holding cells, and this one is the worst. Back at CCA I was in a forty-man cell with two large tanks, one was the sleeping quarters and the other was the dining and entertainment quarter, but there was one guard on duty twenty-four hours per day and they kept the prison population controlled; then I was moved here to Livingston Texas into an eight-man cell, that was not that bad in the sense that I only had to deal with seven other men and most of them were very transient.

But three days ago I was transferred to a different tank, this is a twenty-four man tank, there is no guard in here and this is a big problem. There are five gang members that prey on the weak. I have already made a stand so this is not being taken well by these members because they have lost a small amount of control. The fear currency that they use just lost some of its luster, because I stood my ground against five of them in front of all of the convicts. Everyone in here saw me tell the leader of their group that if he wanted to take my seat he was going to have to do it by force. They all looked at each other and dropped their claim on my seat. That was on my first day in here. They also sleep most of the day and stay awake all night. It's fucking crazy. They sing out loud, play cards, and keep everyone half awake all night.

They also put implants in their penises, they take fragments of dominos and file them down on the floor into any shape they want and then they cut their penises open with a razor knife that was taken out of a shaving razor as contraband and then they shove the piece of domino into the skin of the penis in different locations, the top, sides or bottom of their penis with a toothbrush. I guess they just heal on their own, but I know about this because last night I woke up and saw them doing it, and this morning I asked some of the guys that have been in here with them longer than me. That's how I learned all about it, like I said this place is crazy.

On the third morning in the desert, Lopez finds himself five, maybe ten miles from the California border. He sees cigarette packs, water bottles, tuna cans, McDonald's bags. Trash means people. He knows someone must live nearby. His knees shake. He has barely slept. He has been walking, running, hiding for almost seventy-two hours. Cold at night, sweltering during the day and drinking what water he finds. He can't remember the last time he ate. He has two hours left in him before he'll need to sit down. Dirt covers his torn clothes. He makes his way to a creek. Drinks, bathes, rests. He puts on the pair of clean clothes he brought with him. He starts walking again. He crosses the border but he still sees nothing but desert. He continues walking until he reaches a mobile home community on the outskirts of Dulzura, California, about 12 miles north of Tecate, California. Sun-bleached trailer park homes. Old people tanned almost black. They look at him. He has no plan for this moment, says the first thing that comes to mind.

Good morning. What time is it?

Seven, one woman says.

I'm looking for a phone. I need a mechanic. My car broke down.

We don't have a mechanic no more, a woman told him.

OK, may I use a phone?

We'll call a tow for you. Where'd you break down?

Up the road.

Before or after the checkpoint?

I don't know.

The woman takes a cell phone from her pocket and makes a call. Lopez figures if a tow truck comes, he'll say his car is beyond the checkpoint and catch a ride to where he'll be safe. He's not sure what he'll tell the tow truck driver when he realizes Lopez doesn't have a car.

Tow'll pick you up in 20, 30 minutes, the woman says.

Is there a restaurant around here?

There's a trading post with a place to eat.

She gives him directions, advises him to be careful.

There are a lot of illegals about. Watch it you don't get robbed.

At the trading post, he charges his cell phone. He orders pancakes, fried eggs, chicken fingers, and spaghetti. The waitress stares at him. Lopez ignores her.

Between bites, he calls four cab companies in San Diego but no one wants to drive an hour to Tecate. The fifth company he calls, however, agrees to pick him up for $100.

Forty-five minutes later the cab stops outside the restaurant. The tow truck never showed. Cool. One less thing he'll have to talk himself out of. He gets in the cab and asks the driver to take him to San Diego. At a checkpoint, a border patrol agent stops the taxi and asks for the cab driver's license.

Where you going? he asks Lopez.

Airport.

He stares at the border patrol agent without expression. Airport. It just came to him. Airport. It was the most logical choice. He had money for a ticket. He had ID. He had his credit card. He was exhausted and wanted to get home. He weighed the risks and benefits and saw no risks. No one in the airport would know he was deported. He wasn't flying internationally. His name would not be run through a computer.

No bags? the border patrol agent asks.

No.

Where you going?

Home. Las Vegas.

Why don't you have bags?

I came here with my girlfriend to meet her parents. We got into an argument. I'm going home. Her parents called me a loser. Fuck this. I'm going home.

Yeah, the guard said, shit happens.

He waved the cab through. Lopez slid down in his seat, let out a long breath. If I can fool that motherfucker, I'm good, he tells himself. He sits up, asks the driver to stop at an ATM.

Thank you, he tells the driver. You don't know how you helped me.

At a shopping center ATM, Lopez withdraws $200 and calls Raquel.

I'll pick you up, she says. Don't move. Don't move.

I'm flying, he tells her.

Are you crazy?

Pick me up in Las Vegas.

Houston Detention Center January 18, 2013

It is the age of Aquarius. After all, the beginning of a new era, an era of new life and a prosperous future. But like any new beginning it has its birthing pains, and this is it.

A year after Cesar Lopez's return to the U.S., I drive two days straight from Chicago to Las Vegas to meet him after learning about him through other deported vets. I knock on the door of a white house on a street cramped with white houses paled even whiter by the desert sun, but instead of Lopez, I get his sister, Raquel. It's clear I'm not expected. Raquel just stares at me. I introduce myself but my name means nothing. I ask for Cesar. The sun beats down.

"I could use a glass of water," I tell her.

"Let me call Cesar," she says.

Minutes later, she lets me in, apologizes. She reached Lopez and he confirmed my appointment. I ask for water again. Raquel goes into the kitchen. I hear a faucet running.

"Cesar doesn't trust people," Raquel says, walking out of the kitchen with a glass of water. "So when he meets someone he doesn't know, he sends them here so he can check them out. He didn't tell me you were coming."

Lopez shows up in a white pickup about 20 minutes later. He walks into Raquel's house, ignores me. He tells her son he'll teach him how to ride a motorbike. Raquel introduces us, says, "Why didn't you tell me he was coming?" Lopez looks at me for the first time, laughs, shrugs it off.

Sits in a chair, sinks down, legs sprawled out before him. He looks at me again. No, "Hi," or "Nice to meet you." Yet I can tell he's checking me out. The sidelong glance, the way he pauses and stares at the floor and in the silence takes in my presence.

"Let's eat," he says.

The next morning, I meet Lopez at his place.

He and Fabiola live in a one-bedroom apartment about a thirty-minute drive from Raquel's house. Fabiola likes dogs and they have three, two schnauzers and a bulldog. The bulldog stays in its cage, even when they are both home from work. It rubs against the cage, grunts like a pig when I walk in. Lopez says it will "ripshit" the two other dogs but it seems friendly enough to me, if a little wound up.

A flat-panel TV takes up most of the living room. Off to one side, a shelf filled with DVDs and CDs. A photograph of Lopez graduating from Western Technical College lists against photos of his mother and two daughters. A black-and-white photo of his godmother in Juarez stands off to one side.

He lets the dogs out on the deck to piss, hoses it down after they finish. He'd walk them but he's not supposed to have dogs and worries a neighbor might rat him out. He won't live scared but he won't be stupid. His wife adores the dogs. Stupid to tempt fate, bring attention to themselves. She's not a citizen either. Maybe they'll move. Yeah, it might be time.

He leads the bulldog to his cage in the bedroom. The morning sunlight reveals a hole in the wall above the bed where Lopez laid a punch to alert the neighbor above them he was playing his music too fucking loud. Framed pictures of busty comic book heroines posed provocatively hang above a desk with a computer. Lopez digs the shit out of comic books. Comic books kept him out of LA gangs. He wears a belt buckle with the insignia of the Flash.

"I'm more of the Punisher than I am the Flash," Lopez says, referring to a cartoon character created in 1974 who employs murder, kidnapping, extortion, coercion, threats of violence, and torture in his war on crime. "But I joined the Marines because of Captain America."

"Why the Punisher?"

"In LA, I was obsessed with death," he says. "I wasn't involved in it but I was around it all the time."

Lopez introduces me to Fabiola. She stands over the stove boiling water for coffee, dressed in a blue waitress uniform ready to leave for work. Thirty years old but looks younger. She tells me that when she first saw Lopez after he crossed he looked exhausted but happy. March 16, 2013. Raquel had brought him to his mother's house after his plane landed in Las Vegas. He was sitting down. He looked so skinny. Fabiola said nothing. She just hugged him and wept. They had not seen one another since he had left for Costa Rica almost a year earlier.

She sent a letter to me and says she loves me, Lopez wrote of Fabiola in one of his last diary entries. She likes that I cry at Disney cartoons and curse like a sailor at baseball games without flinching. She likes that I feed the homeless when we go out and she likes that I complain when she asks me to fix the car but end up doing it anyway.

Lopez and Fabiola stayed with his mother for three months because Fabiola had sold their furniture and bedroom set while he was detained to raise money for a lawyer. Lopez got mad about that.

I'm sorry, she told him. I had to get money.

He is a different man now, Fabiola tells me. More serious, attentive. He cooks, helps her around the house, anything to please her. After he was deported, some of her friends told her, Why wait for him? You're young, leave him. It wasn't like that, she told them. We're married. Married for good and bad. God gave them some bad. She had to deal with it.

Fabiola tries not to think about Lopez being deported again. If she did, she would not enjoy life. If it happens, they'll pack all their things and leave together. All these problems are the consequences of what he did when he was young. It will never end.

Lopez looks at his watch. He's off today from his restaurant job but he promised a friend he'd install her ceiling fan. Handyman work. Make a little money on the side. Restaurant doesn't pay much. Some people tip well. Others not so much. Cheap fucks. Sometimes Lopez travels to comic book conventions to earn a little money. Sells prints he has collected of different characters. Chesty heroines. Guys love them. Sometimes he makes $700 in a week selling prints, other times just $100. Whatever, he enjoys it.

We leave Lopez's apartment, pile into his pickup. The Styrofoam tray filled with leftovers from last night's dinner takes up the passenger seat. Lopez tosses it in the back seat, says he thought I took it back to my hotel. I shake my head. Got a feeling it's going to stay back there until he throws it away.

Turning out of the apartment parking lot, we head down narrow streets lined with parked cars and one-story white houses damp-shined from dew. The knotty grass in the small lawns blink with small clouds of bugs dancing in the spray from sprinklers. The sun flares across the windshield and I shield my eyes as Lopez slips on sunglasses.

His ID is still good, driver's license still valid. Not sure what he'll do when it expires. Drive very mindful of the speed limit, he supposes. He anticipates getting caught and being deported again. He had nightmares for weeks and weeks after he returned to Las Vegas and still dreams of the border agents catching him, kicking down doors or stopping him at the border. A few times he dreamed he had died on the mountain. He would get drunk to sleep. He was so tired he couldn't walk. His legs were in constant pain from three days of walking, and he needed Fabiola to help him stand his first week back. When he was able to get around, his father-in-law got him the restaurant job. He has a small pot belly now. He pats his stomach and smiles.

He saves his money so he and Fabiola will be prepared when that "dark day" arrives and immigration agents come for him. He plans to stay in Vegas three years. If he still can't clean up his citizenship thing, he and Fabiola will move to Mexico on their own. Maybe open a restaurant. Crazy to think about. All he wanted to do in Mexico was get back home. He loves America but America doesn't love him back is how he sees it. Like a bad divorce. There's no reconciliation happening. His life has been erased. He doesn't exist in the U.S. anymore. Yes, he made mistakes. Then he made a course correction. Then he got snagged at Houston International Airport.

We pull into the driveway of a flat-roofed home with piles of discarded furniture in the front yard. The home belongs to Sherry Rose. Miss Sherry Baby, as Lopez calls her. She is a sixty-six-year-old nurse who met Lopez at Lindo Michoacan. Her home flooded from rain, and she was remodeling the entire house. Wiring, the floors, everything. She didn't know how to do any of that shit, she told Lopez. I do, he said. He began working for her when he was off from the restaurant.

One day at her house, Lopez got to talking about his life. He said he was a Marine. How crazy is that, Sherry thought.

Her ex-husband had been in Vietnam. They talked about what soldiers go through. He told her he didn't have papers. She didn't care. Her son-in-law doesn't have papers. He's from Guatemala, she said.

"Miss Sherry Baby, I'm here," Lopez announces, letting himself into the house. We walk through a narrow hall into the empty living room. Lopez looks at the bare walls mildewed from damp. A box with a ceiling fan stands on the floor near the bare fireplace. Paint cans, rollers, trays, rags. Lopez runs his hand along the walls, feeling them for texture, determining where he has to sand and smooth them. He decides to paint the living room walls and install the fan.

"How long will you be here today?" Sherry shouts, her voice approaching us until she emerges from a hall. Short. Plastic jewelry hanging from her wrists. You got bling, Lopez teases her.

"I'm going to start in the hall today," he says.

"Sounds good. You going to put a fan in there?"

"I'll fix this one first. Do I have stuff to fix in the dining room?"

"Yes."

A man wanders in, introduces himself. Gary. He'll be working on some plumbing, Sherry says. She asks us if we want coffee and steps into the kitchen to make some.

"Gary is on bail for vehicular manslaughter," Lopez says of the twenty-eight year old plumber. "You just met someone with more problems than me. I'm thinking of submitting an application to the pope to canonize Miss Sherry Baby. She's always picking up sad cases."

"That's true," Sherry says from the kitchen. "How old were you, Lopez, when you acted stupid?"

"Twenty-six. Forty-four now."

"OK. You're allowed to be stupid in America. I can be stupid, and I won't get deported."

Lopez struggles to install a ceiling fan in Miss Sherry Baby's living room. It keeps wobbling. He doesn't know why.

"What's the problem?" she asks. "Can't even it out?"

"I'm trying to make it more stable. Need to put in a washer. Might need two washers."

His older daughter is messing up, he tells Miss Sherry Baby. She didn't complete the paperwork for tuition assistance at the University of Texas. I need five thousand dollars, she told him. Am I bailing you out of jail? he asked. No, to pay for college. I didn't fill out the financial aid forms. Welcome to the adult world, he said. If that's the reason, live and learn. Go to community college. She did. Now she wants him to pay her car registration. Need to look for a part-time job if you need to register your car, he told her. She got mad and hasn't called him in a while. He figures he'll talk to her again when she needs something else.

"OK, that's good," Lopez says of the fan, its blades turning evenly.

"You seen Patrick?" Sherry asks about a mutual friend.

"I'm fixing his boiler."

"What's wrong?"

"Leak."

Lopez stretches. He hears Gary in the other room. Gary might get sent up for manslaughter, but he won't be deported. It almost came to that a few weeks before I arrived. Lopez was driving his motorcycle and got in a fight with a guy he accused of trying to run him over. He popped the guy good and the guy dropped to the ground, TKO, motherfucker. That should have ended it but then the guy's girlfriend got out of the pickup and started chasing Lopez, calling him all kinds of cuss words. The guy gets up, bleeding. Lopez tried to pick up his bike but was too busy running from the girlfriend and trying to hold himself back and not hit her. Sure enough, the cops showed up and ran his license. All of his information came up.

You were deported?

Yes.

And you're a Marine.

Yes.

I'm a Marine myself. Let me talk to my partner.

He spoke to the other officer. Together they spoke to the guy and his girlfriend. Lopez picked up his motorcycle. The cop walked back to Lopez.

The guy is pressing charges.

Yeah!

Yeah, but he'll drop his charges if you drop yours.

OK, Lopez said.

Good luck, Marine,

"Life would be a lot easier if I could just become someone else," Lopez tells me.

"Do you think you're a little self-destructive?" I ask him.

"No, man," Lopez says. "I just won't live scared."

His actions confuse me. He is not like other people I've written about. Lopez is different. Sometimes I applaud him; sometimes I want to yell at him; sometimes I feel he's disloyal; sometimes I think he would do anything for America; sometimes I think he only cares about himself. He can be cocky, and yet he cries. And these feelings he generates in me are the same feelings he experiences dealing with the government. He loves the U.S., but hates the laws. He loves the Marines, but wants to do things his way. He wants the law to respect him, but seems able to break laws without remorse. He seems ambitious enough to reach a place that will make him happy, but I wonder. He is a bundle of exasperating contradictions, frustrated by his own behavior and a system set up to provide order and control. But Lopez won't be controlled.

Lopez gathers his tools. He tells Miss Sherry Baby that he will be back on his next day off from the restaurant. A Marine working in a fucking restaurant. He could have gotten a job doing electrical work, but that kind of thing, usually requires a background check. He didn't need to have his name pop up. Oh, well. Fabiola works in a restaurant, too. She's from Guadalajara. She lived with ten people in a one-bedroom apartment when she reached Las Vegas. That's the standard for immigrants. Lopez would like a better job, but he hasn't been able to penetrate what he calls the "wetback network." He shows up and the Mexicans on the street corner look him up and down and figure him to be undercover. Maybe because he still walks with a military strut. Maybe because he speaks English. They tell him he scares away employers.

He thinks that growing up in LA made him a very different person than he really is at heart. He doesn't see himself as violent or mean. Cocky, maybe. He won't put up with nonsense. Why should he? Maybe he's just a failure as an American and needs to find his place in the world. But what's more American than to be a Marine? He wants to enjoy life the way he sees all his friends enjoying life. He is happy with his wife and dogs. He is happy when his daughters spend time with him. He is happy with his family. He watched his nephew's wedding in El Paso via Skype recently. He had been invited to attend but he won't ever visit Texas again.

Sometimes he thinks of his father. He still wanders into shady bars like he did as a kid half expecting to see him. The old man's been dead a long time.

For a while, Lopez says, he had a hero complex. He'd try to protect people, stand up for them. Like trying to help out Rudy by introducing him to the Juarez drug dealer, Nazario. Where'd that get him? Got him shit, that's where. He's more selective now. Miss Sherry Baby, now she's different. She's the kind of person he'll help. People like her define America, he says. He'd like to go somewhere without someone on his back, find a community filled with Miss Sherrys. But his wife now is in family mode. Wants kids. There's always something.

We leave Miss Sherry Baby's house and get in his truck. He's got to get on and help Patrick. He drives slowly but in his mind he tells me he is racing time before he gets that knock on the door. He needs to straighten out his shit. He talked to a lawyer not long ago. He said he could fix Lopez's case for forty grand. I guess I'm illegal until I have enough money to make me legal, Lopez told him. Pissed him off.

These days he cries at the memory of walking his mother to the border after she visited him in Tijuana.

See you later, he had said.

When he looks at the mountains outside Las Vegas, he feels himself back in the desert. He feels again the pain in his legs, the stiffness in his body, and he cries at these times, too.

The mountains he sees today, though, are Nevada mountains. U.S. of fucking A. mountains. If he had not joined the Marines he doubts he would have made it. But he did join. He made it home. He made it in the Marines, too. The Corps didn't beat him down. He didn't do half-boot camp because he was a Mexican. According to the law he's still a vet no matter his status as a citizen. He wanted to re-enlist after 9/11 but the Marine Corps didn't want him because of his other than honorable discharge. Another opportunity denied. He didn't put up with other people's shit, bottom line. His discharge can be upgraded to honorable if he files an appeal.

He laughs to himself and shakes his head. "Life is strange, isn't it?" he says. He had heard about the 1996 immigration law when it was passed by Congress. All Mexicans are hip to

new immigration laws, he says. But he didn't think it applied
to him. He had his green card. He thought that made him a
citizen.

"A boy loves his parents," he tells me. "Then he screws up,
and his parents tell him to move out. What happened to that
love between them? It doesn't go away. The U.S. put me out.
But I still love my country."

At his apartment, Lopez parks and walks me to my car.
Two days with Lopez and now it's time for me to head back
to Chicago. He asks how I'll go, the route. He wants to drive
somewhere, step on the gas, and roll. Like Jack Kerouac and
Neal Cassady. Like me now. But unlike me, if he gets a ticket he'll be deported. Africa, Mexico, Costa Rica. Shit. Some
place.

"Keep moving," he tells me, but he is really speaking to
himself.

Burial Rites

W e sit at a round table in the cool of a house with wood floors and a wide living room scattered with dog crates. Behind the crates, sliding glass doors open to a back yard patchy with grass and dusty from the play of dogs and the oven-like-heat of El Paso.

Clavo Martinez and his wife, Rosemary, live here. They operated an animal shelter some years ago and took 100 pit bulls off the street. They even found themselves rescuing lizards and ferrets. At that point, they decided running an animal shelter was overwhelming and shut it down. But they kept eleven dogs that were too damaged to adopt out, among them an Australian Cattle Dog, a Red Heeler, that had been hit by a car and a chihuahua with liver problems.

"Man or animal," Clavo says, "you shouldn't die alone."

Clavo is fifty years old and a large man with the rolling gait of a bear. Here in the kitchen, he folds his arms across his chest and leans back, his body consuming the chair. He

adjusts his glasses and runs a big hand through his black
hair. Despite his size, he has a soft voice that grows sharp
when he speaks of something that arouses his passions.
From an envelope, he pulls out a photograph of young man
in a military uniform. The man has thick black hair, heavy
eyebrows, and a heavy black mustache. His gaze strays toward his left shoulder. An American flag hangs behind him.

"This is him?" I ask.

"Yeah, that's Manuel de Jesus Castano," Clavo says.

I consider the photo. Castano was a soldier in the Army
and a deported vet. He died in Mexico but because he was
honorably discharged he remained eligible for benefits, including burial with full military honors. After he died, his
family received a certificate from President George W. Bush
commemorating Castano's "selfless consecration to the
service of our country in the Armed Forces of the United
States." The Texas state Senate issued a proclamation in
which it called Castano a man of "courage, strength and
compassion." The Senate extended "sincere condolences to
the bereaved family of Manuel De Jesus Castano."

I heard about Castano from Hector Barajas-Varela in
Tijuana. He had his name and those of other deceased de-
ported veterans taped to a wall by his desk in the Bunker.
If I wanted to know Castano's story, contact Clavo, Barajas-
Varela told me. I did, and a few weeks after we spoke by
phone I drove to El Paso.

"The day I got the call about him was May 2012, and I
was driving toward UTEP," Clavo continues, referring to the
University of Texas at El Paso.

He had an appointment with his adviser. He had just
turned his car onto Montana Avenue when his cell phone
rang. One of those typical southwest Texas mornings. The
cool of the desert was fast ratcheting up into a hard heat.

Neighborhoods buzzed with the steady hum of air conditioning units and cars in the distance appeared elevated on wavy heat lines.

The man on the phone introduced himself: Luis Ortiz. He sounded frantic and spoke quickly, Clavo recalls. Luis's uncle Manuel de Jesus Castano had died in a Juarez hospital just across the border from El Paso. Luis had gotten Clavo's name from Barajas-Varela, whom he had heard about from his uncle and tracked down on the internet. Barajas-Varela told Luis there was little help he could offer him from Tijuana. He offered him the same advice he offered me: call Clavo.

Clavo was a vet himself. Desert Storm. Gung-ho patriotic. He continued saluting the flag after he returned home. Put his hand on his chest to say the Pledge of Allegiance, the whole bit. He was proud of his service, proud of his country. What do they say in the Army? "Don't ask questions. Do."

His wife was surfing Facebook one day when she came across Barajas-Varela's Facebook page full of stories about deported vets. Have you heard of this? she asked Clavo.

Veterans can be deported? Clavo said.

They are being deported, Rosemary said.

There was probably something else going on with deported vets that he didn't know about, Clavo thought. The government would not just deport them. Still, as a vet and a man proud of his Mexican heritage, the idea stayed in his mind.

Two years later in 2011, Clavo, an engineer with a freight railway company, had a head-on collision with another train after its engineer moved it onto the track Clavo was using. Clavo saw its headlight. He jumped out before the trains collided and blew out his right knee in the fall. Laid up, off work with a disability claim, Clavo had time on his hands. He did a lot of reading on the internet, much of it critical of the U.S. and its use of military power. It got Clavo thinking: Why do we go to war? What are soldiers dying for? What was the real purpose of Desert Storm?

He followed Rosemary's lead and began reading Facebook posts on deported vets. They do a stretch in prison and then are put out on the streets in a country they haven't seen since they were kids? Wasn't that punishing them twice? And they're doing this to vets? How could he be proud of his service when this was happening to vets? He and Rosemary began messaging Barajas-Varela to learn more.

Although he established a rapport with Barajas-Varela, Clavo never fully grasped the consequences of deporting veterans until Luis called him and he was confronted with one family's loss. Luis told him that his uncle Manuel Castano had been sick. Doctors had given him blood transfusions, but nothing worked and he died. His family wanted to bring his body home.

"What kind of funds do you have?" Clavo asked.

Very little, Luis told him. The family was pulling together as much money as possible but Luis worried it would not be enough.

Clavo heard the distress in Luis's voice. All the pressure he was feeling taking on this task for his family. The oldest nephew. The man accepting responsibility without knowing what to do.

Clavo did not know what he could do to help either but said he'd mention Castano at the American GI Forum that night. The Forum is the nation's largest Hispanic veterans' organization chartered by Congress. Clavo promised to call Luis afterward.

The highway from Clavo's house to the home of Luis Ortiz snakes its way through the desert, past outposts of mini-malls and gas stations and incomplete housing developments that dead end at barren expanses of scrub brush and sand.

Luis leads me into his living room and we sit at a table. He is thirty-nine but looks younger. He seems a little uncertain about his uncle, a little self-conscious discussing him, aware, I'm sure, of some of the unsavory details of his life. He tells me he never saw his uncle Manny in his Army uniform. But his uncle had told him he had traveled the world.

Military service was in the family's blood. Luis is an Army supply sergeant. "I'm the guy who denies stuff," he says and laughs. Three of his four uncles had joined the military and four of his cousins, too. One uncle was wounded in Desert Storm. He lives alone and doesn't talk to the rest of the family much. All of his uncles except Manny were citizens when they joined. After he was deported, Castano told Luis he had thought he'd get his papers through the military.

Luis does not know why his uncle joined the Army, other than because enlisting in the service was always something the men in his family did. Luis enlisted because of his uncles. One uncle who was in charge of recruiting in El Paso advised him to study helicopters. Be a crew chief, he said. Luis should have listened. Instead, he went into the infantry, straight grunt. His uncle told him, you should have listened to me. He also said, if the higher-ups get to you and you want to leave, they've succeeded. Don't let them get to you.

If it were not for the military, Luis's uncles might have been farm workers like their parents. Luis shows me brown, grainy photos of them in the fields, squinting before the camera, adults in straw hats with children huddling beside them. Everyone holds a hoe, the farm field divided into rows of what looks like cabbage stretching far behind them.

Before suburban sprawl consumed El Paso, you could pick jalapeños and watermelon right outside the city, Luis says. The family would get together at his grandparents' house in Asherton, Texas, and work the fields around Del

Rio and Lubbock. As a kid, Luis would hand out water and burritos to the adults out picking. They'd start at 3 a.m. and stay out late. His uncle Manny worked hard.

Castano left the Army in 1984 and returned to El Paso, where most of the family lived. His service had not granted him citizenship. Years of wandering followed. He was picked up for domestic violence and public intoxication.

Luis last saw him in 2008. He was healthy, a big guy. Luis remembers barbecues with him. The music and laughter. His uncle always had music playing. He didn't drink in front of the family or on someone else's property. The Castanos were taught manners.

After he was deported, he often called Luis's mother, Maria Gonzalez, from Juarez and asked for clothes. Castano had a Facebook account and would send Luis short messages. He'd talk about the Dallas Cowboys and his son Victor, a Marine in Afghanistan. He told Luis a lot of deported vets lived in Juarez.

What's up mijo? How are you doing . . . when are you coming to Juarez?

Did you watch the Superbowl, mijo?

Doing OK, mijo . . . you know how it is in Juarez . . . but things are looking good for us to come back . . . legally . . . we have a group that is fighting for us to repeal the law for veterans that were deported . . . so that is good news . . .

About sixty or seventy vets gathered in a downtown restaurant for the American GI Forum. At the end of the hour-long meeting, the facilitator asked if anyone had any questions. Clavo stood. He described the phone call he had received from Luis. He said the family was looking for help to bring Castano's body home.

One guy said he would speak to him later.

"Can anyone else help?"

Silence. The meeting adjourned. A few vets walked past Clavo and muttered, Sorry man. The guy who said he'd talk to Clavo after the meeting said he ran a homeless shelter. He asked Clavo to refer people to him. Clavo looked at him. What has that got to do with anything, he wondered. Another vet told him that to bring Castano back would involve too much bureaucracy. The Forum can't take that on, he said.

Clavo stood alone in the restaurant. No one had stepped up. He couldn't believe it. Not even for a fellow vet. Thank you for your help, he said to himself sarcastically. Well, he wasn't going to quit on Castano. He couldn't say, OK, bye. But he also didn't know what else to do.

Clavo told his friend Luis Sarellano, a Vietnam vet, about Castano. Sarellano listened, clasped his hands behind his head, his thinning gray hair tied off in a ponytail. He thought it was crazy, a veteran being deported. Everyone makes mistakes. Some like Castano end up in the justice system. That should not be a reason to be deported, Sarellano said. He thought if you served the country at the very least you should be considered a citizen.

Sarellano, sixty-nine, was born in Mexico. He came to the States as an infant. His parents took him to fields in California to pick cherries. The work could be dangerous. The simplest, most ridiculous things that he would laugh about later could get you hurt. One time when he was twelve, he was up on a ladder holding a tree branch, and the ladder wobbled and slid out from under him. He landed on a branch feet first and it held him long enough to break his fall. He doesn't know how high up he was. High enough to die, if he hadn't landed on the lower branch.

In 1967, Sarellano became a citizen and joined the Navy as a corpsman at the height of the Vietnam War. He chose the Navy because he thought he would be safe aboard a ship most of the time. He didn't know the Marines were part of the Navy and that the Navy provided the medical staff to the Marines in the field.

His command suffered fifty casualties the first time he saw combat. I'm going, one Marine told Luis, I'm not staying. Six weeks later, the guy shot out his right knee with a pistol. He spent ten months in a hospital. It pissed Sarellano off that this guy didn't have to go through the crap he went through. He had a duty just like Luis. He had made a commitment. He had signed an oath to, well, these days, Sarellano is not sure to whom, but he signed it. Then he got out of it. Sarellano didn't. He stayed. He was in Vietnam to do a job and ask questions later, and that's what he did. He returned to the States only when he finished his deployment.

But at the time he didn't know he would come back. He didn't know how long he would live one second to the next. Friends would get killed so often that Sarellano stopped making friends. What was the point? They'd be gone to-morrow. Forty years later he still sees the bodies. He doesn't need photos to remember. He still hears the things he and his fellow soldiers said about dead Vietnamese. The jokes. He feels disgust with himself, the crass comments he made. The Vietnamese had been fellow soldiers. They were brothers. He wonders sometimes how he still sleeps at night.

Two of his sons served in the military: the Air Force and Navy. One of them has post-traumatic stress disorder, as does Sarellano. A son-in-law joined the Army. If he could go back in time, Sarellano would tell them all, don't enlist. Don't do the dirty work for other people. Immigrants do enough of that already. Sarellano's whole family broke their backs since they were old enough to put pants on. He imagines Castano's family was no different.

"Why deport the guy?" he asked Clavo. A man joins the military when he is young, giving the country some of the best years of his life. He deserves to be a citizen. Imagine a guy fighting in Iraq or Afghanistan and then being sent back to where he was born.

"It's unfair," Sarellano said.

Sixty-year-old Maria Gonzalez, remembers her brother as funny and outgoing. Her eyes tear up as she recalls him. She sits at a kitchen table and sometimes stares into space, without revealing her thoughts. Castano was three years her junior, she says. He loved to make jokes. He would scare his three sisters with stories of spiders hanging over their beds. He liked school. He attended Asherton High School and graduated.

Their father worked on a Texas ranch. Maria's mother joked that every time he came to visit them in Mexico, he left her pregnant. When Maria was in the fifth grade, their father brought the family to Texas. Manny must have been in first or second grade then, she says. She remembers crossing the bridge into Laredo all dressed up. Laredo was small and nice. Her mother held her head up, a wide grin on her face. An agent took their fingerprints and gave her mother a paper that he said to keep until they received their permanent alien resident cards.

Her mother always took care of them. She worked so hard. She went house to house giving immunization shots for a clinic. She did a lot of sewing and knitting, too. Her father worked just as hard. He never cussed. He was a very quiet person but strict in his way. If he wanted the children to quiet down, he would make a tsk, tsk, sound and that was it, no more noise. He spoke in a soft whisper. Their mother was the exact opposite. She would shout at the kids. Shout at her husband, too.

As kids, the Castano children worked in the fields. Manuel would cheat a lot, Maria says. They'd work in a line with hoes

and he'd move to the head of the line to get out of work early. Once he chugged a Coke too fast in the heat and passed
out. Their grandmother made tortillas at three in the morning. The kids got to go to high school, but their father picked
them up right after, a big basket of burritos in the backseat to
eat as they drove to the fields. When the children weren't in
school, the family moved around. They hand-planted carrots
in Colorado, cotton in Nebraska, and onions, pickles, and
okra in Florida and Texas.

After high school, Manny enrolled in Southwest Texas
College in Uvalde. He majored in business administration but
wasn't doing very well. He saw his two brothers enlist in the
Army, and he decided to enlist, too. To this day, Maria thrills
at the sight of photographs of her brothers in uniform. The
way they look. So handsome. So full of strength and authority.
She felt excitement when Manuel enlisted. She was so young.
Seeing her three brothers in uniform. It was something. She
can't put it into words what she felt. Something very special.

Castano's discharge papers show that he served in the Army
from 1980 to 1984. He enlisted in San Antonio and attained
the rank of Specialist fourth class. His last duty assignment
was in Europe with the 574th Battalion. He received an
Army Service Ribbon, an Overseas Service Ribbon, a Good
Conduct Medal, a Sharp Shooter Badge with M-16 rifle bar
and an Army Achievement Medal. He accrued fifty-eight
days of paid leave. He separated from the Army at Fort
Jackson, South Carolina.

Clavo also left college for the military, though his troubles
were financial and not academic like Castano's. He left New
Mexico State University and joined the Army Reserves in
1988 to earn the extra money to complete his degree. His

younger brother warned him not to sign up. You know, he said, the U.S. enters a conflict about every ten years.

"Nothing will happen to me," Clavo said. "I'm just doing my eight years."

Two years after he enlisted, Clavo visited his parents in Roswell, N.M. While he was there, news broke that Iraq had invaded Kuwait. Clavo didn't think much of it. He was in the reserves. He wasn't going anywhere. Then on a Saturday morning, three days before Thanksgiving, Clavo's phone rang in his dorm room. A Sgt. Rodriguez shouted at him over the line: We have a roaring bull alert. Pack your bags and be at the reserve center at zero-six-hundred. Roaring bull alert? Clavo thought. Just another exercise, right? But in the back of his mind, Clavo was not so sure. Exercise or not, roaring anything meant you're close to being activated.

Clavo spent Thanksgiving and Christmas in Saudi Arabia. The first days on the ground were the worst, with several incidents of friendly fire. Then Scud missiles hit 200 yards from his post. Gas attack alarms went off 24/7. Everyone was afraid to take their masks off to eat, sleep, do anything. One guy finally had enough. Fuck this, he said, and took his mask off to eat a granola bar. Hey, I'm still here, he said.

Clavo waited for shit to happen. He listened to the explosions of Scud missiles, Patriot missiles. Boom, boom, boom, night and day. Stealth fighters roaring overhead. He would be awake for seventy-two hours straight. The only thing that held his unit together was that all of them, except for two white guys, were Chicano. We're Chicanos too, the white guys said. La Raza. Brown and white, all in the same fucking boat. They watched flashes of light shake the ground, the horizon orange, everything burning.

Clavo returned home in May 1991, married, and moved to El Paso, where Rosemary was from. He was drinking, passing out. He had nerve problems in his hands from exposure to sarin and hauling depleted uranium rounds. In 1997, he was diagnosed with PTSD but the VA did not tell him he could file a disability claim until years later. He continued drinking. The job at the railroad didn't help. The noise of the trains, the smell of diesel took him back to Iraq.

Through good times and bad, no matter whether he was angry or sad, Rosemary stood by him. Had he been undocumented and deported to Mexico with PTSD without Rosemary, without any support of any kind, what would have happened to him?

"They stripped Castano of everything," he says.

One afternoon, Clavo and Rosemary drive me into Juarez to meet deported Navy veteran Juan Valadez at La Nueva Central, a restaurant. Valadez was in touch with Castano shortly after Castano's deportation and tried to help him. Valadez and Clavo are about the same size. Together they squeeze into a booth and laugh as they jostle their bulk into the limited space, much of Clavo leaning out into the aisle. Waitresses rush back and forth in a losing effort to keep up with the numbers of people coming in. Ceiling fans whir, and music overwhelmed by the commotion plays from hidden speakers.

I sit across from Valadez. He has short, dark hair and a trimmed beard. He wears a T-shirt with "Texas" emblazoned across the front. He tells me that he came to Mexico two years before Castano. Valadez had been busted as an accomplice in a scheme to transport 1,000 pounds of pot across state lines. He was out of work at the time and a friend offered to pay him to drive another friend from Dallas to Columbus, Ohio. That was it. Simple. Drop the guy off, done. Valadez knew what he was getting into wasn't legal but he needed the money. He didn't ask questions. The cops stopped his car for speeding and found the pot.

He served a twenty-eight-month prison sentence in Ohio. Then he was transferred to immigration lockup in Seneca County for six months before he was deported to his birthplace, Juarez, in December 2009. His parents had brought him to the States when he was eleven. He had a green card. It never crossed his mind that he could be deported.

Valadez met Varela through Barajas-Varela's deported vets Facebook page. He signed up as a "friend" of the page and soon began reading messages from vets seeking advice for subjects ranging from housing to medical care. They also posted notes about newly deported vets. In August 2011, he read that Castano had been deported to Juarez. Valadez contacted him through Facebook:

> August 2, 2011, 8:43pm
> Juan Valadez
> *Hey I'm also a deported veteran, I'm also living in Juarez, what part of the city are you at?*
>
> Manuel Castano
> *Over on the Colonia Anahuac . . . and you?*
>
> Juan Valadez
> *I live by Plaza Juarez, Im working at ACS, but the truth thats the worst job I've ever had in my life, theres a couple more deported vets working there also.*

He was depressed, Valadez recalls of Castano. At that time, he couldn't find a job. He had applied at construction sites but the foremen weren't hiring. It didn't help that Castano was fifty-four. Age discrimination exists in Mexico too, Valadez says.

Castano told Valadez he had been deported over a drug case. He did not go into specifics and Valadez did not ask.

As far as he was concerned, all deported vets had messed up. But they had done their time. No need to dwell on past mistakes.

Castano was desperate, Valadez thought at the time. He didn't have any money. He said he needed to go to the VA but didn't mention specifics. He was thinking of just crossing back over to the U.S. and getting arrested and locked up again. Better than starving in Juarez, he told Valadez. He was renting a small room by a market that sold electric appliances. He had only a pair of jeans and two shirts. Valadez offered him some old clothes that were still in El Paso but by the time Valadez received the clothes, Castano had died.

Castano wrote to Valadez on Facebook:

I'm tired of this place. Is there a lot of vets where you work at . . . maybe we can get something going to where they can send us some clothes, i have been here 4 months, and i'm struggling, this computer is thanks to a friend of mine that also got deported . . . so let's see what happens.

Valadez knew how tough it was adjusting to a place that will never be your home. You get to Juarez, you have no money, no car, no nothing. Castano had an '83 Volvo but it broke down. Valadez tried to get him work at a call center where he had worked. Castano applied and aced the typing and English tests but the center was laying people off. Castano told the call center he had medical issues. Fifty-four years old with medical issues. He didn't get the job.

Valadez caught a few breaks in Juarez that Castano didn't. After he was deported, Valadez stayed with an uncle. He got the call center job right away. He started a sushi stand in April 2012. There were already a lot of taco and hamburger joints but no sushi. He got enough business that he opened a restaurant.

With the earnings from his restaurant, he enrolled in the Universidad Technologia de Ciudad Juarez. He is studying engineering with an emphasis on renewable energy resources. He married a Mexican woman and now has a five-year-old daughter, Nicole. He will send her to live with his parents in El Paso so she can attend school in the States. The schools are better there, he says, because they provide computer education. The schools in Juarez don't unless you enroll in a private school. Valadez can't afford that. Maybe his daughter can visit him on weekends.

He misses the Navy. He keeps in touch with his Navy buddies on Facebook. Valadez joined right after high school. He had always wanted to be in the service. He was just drawn to it. He was in ROTC and mini boot camp in high school. He and 12 other friends joined the Navy on the same day in 2000. The Navy never mentioned Valadez's status.

For six months he served in the Gulf of Aden between Yemen and Somalia. Special Forces looked for al-Qaida and the Navy provided air support. He received an honorable discharge in 2004.

Valadez married and did not re-enlist.

He and his wife later divorced. He tried getting back into the Navy but he had to lose twenty pounds first. He was trying to lose the weight when he made the choice to drive that guy to Ohio.

"I left the Navy honorably," he says. "I should at least be considered a national."

He never met Castano's family. He remembers Castano telling him he used to live on a ranch that had a fishing pond. He would drink beer and fish and drive his cars, four-wheelers. He didn't go out much. He'd always call Valadez for a job. I'll try to get you in here, Valadez would tell him, but nothing worked out.

"Bad timing," Valadez says.

Castano wrote to him on Facebook:

August 24, 2011, 8:48am
Manuel Castano
I went to ACS yesterday, and I passed everything typed 28 words, in about half a minute, couldn't get started, but still I got 123 on the overall score . . . so just waiting for them to call me, what the heck is CURP . . . they require that also. don't know what that is. so if i get called I'll start Monday . . .

August 24, 2011, 8:29pm
Manuel Castano
I called ACS, today and I was told that I was not accepted, and I had one of the highest scores, I think it's because of my age . . . hell I'm going to keep working construction, and save the 3k and go back illegally, hell these people think that you have to kiss their ass for 250 dollars every two weeks, shit I can make that in a day. . .

Castano also worried about his son Victor, the Marine deployed to Afghanistan. He sent Valadez a messages about him. My son has been in Afghanistan for two weeks . . . I did not get to see him . . . so I feel bad. Valadez told him Victor would be all right.

"Castano was always hopeful of going back to the U.S.," Valadez says. "'I'll go back,'" he'd say. "'It's all bullshit.'"

In their last Facebook exchange, Castano recalled living in Austin.

February 9, 2011
Manuel Castano
How was your new years?

Juan Valadez
It was alright, we went to Samalayuca.

Manuel Castano
Where is that?

Juan Valadez
About an hours drive from Juarez, it's sand dunes we went on the 4-wheelers.

Manuel Castano
Man, I miss that . . . I had two four wheelers and a three wheeler. I have a four acres in Austin with a fishing tank.

Juan Valadez
Thats cool my sister lives in Austin.

Manuel Castano
I lived there for 19 years.

Juan Valadez
Never been but I heard its nice.

Manuel Castano
Man, it is nice . . . that is my home and you are welcomed there.

Valadez felt bad when he read on the deported vets page that Castano had died. Kind of ironic he could finally go home, but only as a dead man. It's just a sad story. Valadez doesn't know of any other way to think about it.

"He didn't speak Spanish well," Valadez tells me. "I never spoke to him in Spanish. He wasn't fluent. He always spoke English. In his mind, he was an American."

Maria says her brother left the service in 1984 and moved to Fort Bliss with his wife, a woman he met while in the Army. They divorced and she died in 2016. They had one son. He started seeing another woman in the late 1980s or early 1990s. They had three children together. Castano was happy. He was working and bought a house in Mexia, a town near Austin.

He didn't talk about his service. He told Maria years later that he still remembered the smell of gunpowder. He and his Army buddies stuck together. That was that. He said little more about the experience.

He loved old cars. He had a yellow pickup, a Corvette Stingray and a black Trans Am, a Smokey and the Bandit kind of thing. The Trans Am had bucket seats. Tex-Mex music blared out of the radio. He was infatuated with the singer María Conchita Alonso. He had posters of her all over the place.

Then Maria lost contact with him, she said. She blames it on the distance from El Paso to Mexia, about a five-hour drive. He would call but would not visit. She says she does not know anything about his arrests but she concedes that his absence may also have been a result of problems with the law. She knows he liked his beer, but she never saw him intoxicated. She never saw him have problems with the police, although he did tell her that he skipped out on going to court on DUI charges a couple of times. She had seen him drink three or four times. He wasn't an angel, she admitted, but he didn't have a drinking problem. He was a good guy, good brother, loved his kids.

Five years passed. Then, in 2005, Maria, her son Raul and her mother began looking for him. The last they knew he was working for a trailer business. They spent the day in Mexia but could not find him. No one knew him. They were getting ready to leave when they stopped at a gas station. Maria was pumping gas when she saw him. A tall, dark complexioned man getting something from the store. Her son was standing next to him. She went inside. Pásale señorita, the man said. At first, she said, he didn't recognize her.

"If you weren't my brother I'd slap you," she said.

Castano laughed, then embraced her warmly. Glancing through the door, he saw their mother and raced out to her. Come to the house, Castano told them. They stayed and ate dinner. Manuel had a perpetual grin on his face, she says. He worked building U-Haul trucks. He seemed happy. He had gone to Mexico and returned.

He moved back to El Paso in 2007 when their older brother Nicholas was diagnosed with Lou Gehrig's disease. He had split up with the woman in Mexia. He stayed with Maria for two weeks, and then moved in with his dying brother. He painted houses. Around 2010 he moved in with a woman. He didn't know her that well and didn't live with her long. They'd drink. The woman would call Maria. Pick him up, she'd say. I can't have my kids around him.

That same year, Maria says, he called her from an ICE holding facility. Said he needed his reading glasses. She asked him what happened.

You know, he said.

No, I don't.

He told her that the authorities had asked him if he wanted to go to jail or be deported. It is up to you, your decision, they said.

I don't want to go to jail for a DUI and a speeding ticket, he told them.

Maria said Manuel had liked Juarez at first and traveled all around the city. He stayed with a deported friend. But he had no job, no money, and his enjoyment of the city soon vanished.

Can you help me? he'd ask his sister. I need food, clothes, shoes.

What Maria didn't know at the time was that Castano's deportation resulted from a history of criminal convictions. On October 18, 2002, he had received a ten-year prison sentence for injury to a child and failure to appear in court in Hays County, Texas. Injury to a child can include a variety of offenses against children under the age of fourteen from negligence to intentional conduct, and minor injuries to serious injuries up to and including death. He was paroled on July 23, 2003.

"I have no personal recollection of the case, which was originally prosecuted in 1993 by a prosecutor who no longer works in the district attorney's office," said Wes Mau, the district attorney of Hays County.

According to ICE, Castano was deported in September 2003. An ICE spokesman said that the agency assumes Castano returned to Texas illegally because on June 15, 2010, he began serving an eight-month sentence for fraudulent use and possession of false identification in Limestone County, Texas. He was paroled under mandatory supervision on March 25, 2011. He was deported again the same month.

"His criminal convictions—including two DUIs, felony child abuse and felony identity theft—made him an ICE enforcement priority," the spokesman told me in an email. ICE, he said, "specifically identifies service in the U.S. military as a positive factor that should be considered when deciding whether or not prosecutorial discretion should be exercised."

Clavo has dreams of running from people and hiding behind rocks. He wants to kill someone but he has only his sidearm and it won't fire. He wakes up. He takes meds to help him sleep but nothing stops the dreams.

In Iraq it seemed he was always hiding and moving to protect everyone else. He served in an evac hospital with Eighteenth Corps, Army Airborne. One day, some nurses wanted to build a bunker to save lives from incoming fire. Engineers dug a huge pit with a backhoe. They put a long-ass board over it.

Let's see how many people fit in there, the commander said. They got in, packed tight shoulder to shoulder, butt to butt. This is just a grave, someone said, and they all jumped out. Clavo thinks of that, how they all just piled in without thinking. Fucking lemmings, man.

He wonders what Castano experienced, what things might have haunted him about his service. Clavo sees images of burned bodies and smells death mixed with burning oil wells. Overwhelming. Oil and bodies, oil and bodies.

Clavo, two other guys, and a nurse went AWOL for two days. They walked to an amusement park. People loitered around a carnival. Clavo thought they looked just like him. The same skin color, dark hair, everything. He had never thought, I'm fighting people who look just like me and may be as poor as me. He watched kids on a Ferris wheel and an old guy with prayer beads. Clavo had a set of prayer beads, too. They looked cool so he had bought them. The old man offered him black tea. Strong with sugar. They talked without understanding each other. The old man shook his hand.

Clavo remembers the fear he felt when a letter from the VA arrived that would tell him if he would receive disability for his PTSD. He didn't want to know if something was wrong him. He knew a Vietnam era vet, Al Soto, who used to walk all over town. He was found dead in his apartment after he got his letter.

Clavo opened the envelope. The VA concluded he should be classified as totally disabled. You'll get this much money but you'll never work again, the letter read. He hit rock bottom. Why go back to school? Why do anything? Who'll hire him? It took him a while to get out of his depression.

He doubts anyone looks at him and thinks, Oh, that guy is screwed up mentally. He wonders again what problems Castano may have had. If he can remember Castano, then maybe other people will remember him, too. A vet should not be forgotten, no matter his problems. As a soldier, Castano swore to serve and protect. That should count for something. Clavo has talked to a few people about him. Some actually gave a damn.

Manuel Castano never told Maria he was sick until she saw him in the hospital. He was joking even then.

A man who worked with Castano in construction called her in May 2012. Your brother Manuel is sick and he won't see the doctor, the man said. He'll call you later on. Tell him to see a doctor.

Castano called later that day. I'm not sick, he said. I'm just dehydrated. Take care.

A few days later, the same man called.

Your brother is in the hospital.

What happened?

I don't know.

Which hospital?

Seguro Social Hospital.

She didn't know the hospital or how to get to it. A friend's husband took her from El Paso to Juarez. The hospital was something else, she recalls. Ugly. A place you'd go to die. Filthy. The smell like an intense heat, enough to make you melt, enough to shut your lungs. All the people with no money go there, her friend's husband told her.

A woman led her to intensive care. They told her to put on a gown, a cap, and plastic gloves. Oh, my God, what is going on, Maria wondered. Then they led her in. She saw Castano on a bed beneath a sheet, beeping machines on either side of him. She leaned over her brother.

"Manuel," she said.

He smiled.

"What's wrong with you?"

The sheet covered only his stomach. She noticed black bruises on his legs down to his toes.

"What's wrong?"

"Nothing."

"No, you're sick."

"Nothing is wrong," he said.

"What happened to your legs?"

"Nothing, just bruises."

"Those are big bruises."

"It's nothing."

A nurse stopped and asked what he wanted to eat.

"Steak."

The nurse smiled.

"I can't. You might choke. I can bring you Jell-O."

Then, turning to Maria, the nurse said, "The doctor needs to talk to you in his office. I'll take you."

Maria followed her down a long, dank hall.

"Do you know that your brother has Lou Gehrig's Disease? Does anyone in your family have it?"

"My father," Maria said, "and an older brother."

"Well, it is very advanced. It's gone up to his chest."

"What can we do?"

"We need blood for a transfusion and medicine."

The doctor gave her a prescription. Maria understood she would have to buy his medication and pay for the transfusion.

The nurses would not let her stay overnight. You have to wait outside in the waiting room, they said. "We'll let you know when you can see him again." Children vomited on the floor around her. She left. She had a job at Kmart. Her supervisors said, "Don't worry. Whenever you have to go to see your brother, go. It's OK."

Maria returned to Juarez the next day. Castano didn't talk to her. He behaved as if he did not recognize her. A nurse told her to talk to him anyway. He can hear you, she said. Castano pressed her hand. His eyes were closed.

"What happened?" she asked the doctor.

"The disease is progressing."

She visited daily. One time, when she left the hospital, she walked around Juarez and got lost. She looked at all sorts of buildings with gates. I don't know where I am, she thought. The street signs meant nothing to her. She called a friend to pick her up.

Days passed. Castano stopped eating. Fluid dripped into his right arm from an IV. He needs blood, the doctor said. Maria began paying for transfusions. The nurses still would not let her stay with her brother. She stuck around the hospital, waiting to be allowed to see him again. When she could put up with the foul odors, she sat in the waiting room. Other times, she paced outside. She had no idea what the doctors were doing. It was stressful, not seeing him. She knew it was bad.

More days folded into one another, dominoing forward. One morning she could not find her brother. He wasn't in his hospital room. She asked almost a dozen people, where's my brother?

A doctor showed her to a room on the second floor. That's him, the doctor said. Her brother looked shrunken and impossibly small, Maria recalls. I don't think he's going to make it, she remembers thinking. She spoke to him. He squeezed her hand. The doctor wouldn't let her stay.

"I'll be back," she said. The next morning she drove to work and the doctor called to say he had died.

She returned to Juarez. She felt guilty that she had not
been with him when he died. When the doctor had asked her
to pay for the blood transfusion she had known then it would
be a miracle if he survived. And if he had, what then? What
would she have done if the doctor told her, You have to take
him home? Quit her job and take care of him around the
clock? How would she have supported her family? Manuel
would have suffered. He wouldn't have wanted that. If he
hadn't been in Mexico, maybe he would have lasted longer.
Her father went through a lot but he was in the U.S. and lasted a long time. She wondered how she would tell her mother.

At the hospital, the doctors took her to his room where
he lay dead, eyes open to the ceiling. Maria closed his eyes.
The hospital gave her his wallet. There was nothing in it except his Mexican ID. He also had a Bible and his discharge
papers. The hospital told her it needed $16,000 to release his
body. She felt as if someone had just punched her hard in
the stomach. She couldn't breathe. Sixteen thousand dollars?
Where would she get that kind of money? She struggles to
get by. Her life isn't easy, she says. People think it's easy for
immigrants. It's not.

"We can't release the body without the money," she was
told. "We can bury him in a common grave."

"What can I do?"

"You have to pay something and then sign a contract to
pay the rest. Ask your family."

"They are doing what they can do."

She returned home and pawned all of the jewelry that she
had. Her children gave her money. Her son Luis made phone
calls asking for help but got nowhere. Maria managed to pull
together $3,200. She hoped the hospital would work with her.

A friend told her, "Don't tell them you have this money.
Offer them $50 and negotiate."

"But they won't give me his body."

Her son Luis said, "Tell them you only have $300."

"OK."

"You were buying all his meds," Luis said. What more do they want?"

Maria returned to the hospital. She decided against negotiating with the hospital. She wanted her brother's body released so she could bury him. So he could rest in peace. She offered the hospital all of the money that she had collected. The hospital administrator, she recalls, didn't hesitate. He accepted the payment without question or reference to the $16,000 he had originally demanded. The man just wanted whatever she would give him. Other people would want her money, too. To pay for the transfer, plot, and burial of her brother, she would ask her family to contribute.

"He probably didn't expect that much," she says now.

Maria's son, Luis, told Clavo the family had raised enough money to take control of the body. He told Clavo he would get back to him about a church service for his uncle. Meanwhile, the body was transferred to a Juarez funeral home. The San Jose Funeral Home in El Paso agreed to coordinate with the authorities in Mexico so the body could be removed to Texas. Maria paid the Juarez funeral home $500 and the director said he would put Castano in a cardboard casket. Bring black socks and a suit to dress him, the director said. On a Sunday, the San Jose Funeral Home called.

"The body is here," they told Maria.

Her friends chided her for spending so much money, but what else could she have done? She didn't want her brother buried in Mexico. He had been unhappy in Juarez. It was hot and violent. No, he would not have wanted to be buried there.

Maria had kept the news of Castano's death from her mother until she knew his body would be sent back. Now, she needed to tell her. She asked her two nieces to be with her when she spoke to her mother. You be strong, she told her mother. You can't get sick on me here. You have to be strong for me.

A funeral mass was held at St. Peter and Paul Church in El Paso. Just family and a few friends. A friend of Castano who had worked with him on some Juarez construction projects approached Maria. She can't recall his name. He was a man Castano had lived with for a while. One day, the man told her, he had asked Castano for a measuring tape. Castano attempted to throw it but dropped it instead. That was a while ago, the man said. He was sick even then.

Maria had always thought her brother would cross the bridge connecting Juarez to El Paso and return to the States. He'll beat this, she thought. He'll come back. He did, finally, but not the way she expected.

His death was a relief. He's close now and Maria can visit him. She just wanted him to have what he deserved.

Renwick Dozier, the director of the San Jose Funeral Home on Virginia Street in El Paso, served in the Army from 1974 to 1994. He was discharged with the rank of sergeant first class.

He and I speak by phone. He comes across as a gentle soul who feels badly for every family that comes to him suffering from loss. His deep voice has a soothing tone, and although I was not coming to him to arrange a funeral, I felt he was reaching out to me anyway as if to say should I need him he would be there for me.

When Maria called about her brother, he told her as long as he was honorably discharged he was eligible for burial at

Fort Bliss. He had handled many body transfers from Mexico to Texas. It wasn't uncommon. He thought a burial at Fort Bliss was Castano's right. He wasn't coming back to the U.S. to live but to be interred by his family. Renwick is grateful to all veterans, no matter what mistakes they may have made after their service.

He remembers some delays because of Castano's status as a deportee. The U.S. and Mexican consulates had to talk to one another. The U.S. consulate offered some resistance. The people there didn't realize he was eligible for a military funeral.

Renwick's first thought was, He's a vet. He didn't care about Castano's status. Whatever mistakes he made, he was still a vet. Vets are a brotherhood in and of themselves.

"Whether you served two years or thirty," Renwick says. "You're still a veteran. All vets understand that."

While I am in El Paso I try to reach Castano's son Victor, but I am unsuccessful. Finally, we connect through Facebook and arrange a time for me to call him. A photo on Facebook shows him in his Marine uniform. His grandmother is handing him the flag that had draped his father's coffin. Victor appears to be holding back tears, his face strained and about to crumble. His grandmother, too, looks distraught.

On the phone, he speaks in a low, flat voice that rarely rises or falls. He is direct. But what feelings he has, he conceals. Or they've all drained away long ago from his time in Afghanistan.

In 2008, Victor tells me, he saw his father Manuel Castano for the last time. Victor had joined the Marines and was in boot camp. Boot camp was easy. His father had taught him what to expect. Don't talk back. Listen. Take orders. They're given for a reason, his father had told him. Do it. Don't ask questions.

His father jumped around a lot from job to job. It seemed
he did a little bit of everything. He never talked about the
Army but he was always proud of having been a soldier. It is
something you carry forever, Victor says. He doesn't know if
his father saw combat. He knows that his service affected his
life. But his father wouldn't talk about it. Instead, he laughed
and smiled. You can be in a shitty situation but you can still
look at the bright side of things, Victor says. He remembers
being shot at in Afghanistan, lying in holes, explosions going
off around him. He remembers the hungry kids he saw over
there. He doesn't talk about his service either. He has PTSD.
His unit was hit by quite a few IEDs. He looks at every single
person and doesn't let his guard down.

"You risk changing who you are because you want to
serve your country," he says.

His father thought it was his country. He was good at
masking his feelings. He was always that way. Now, Victor is
too. In his head a million things are going on but at the end
of the day Victor just wants to be happy. He could have died.
Every day in Afghanistan might have been his last. He had
no guarantees he would be here tomorrow.

Whether his father saw combat or not doesn't matter to
Victor. His father is still a vet. It is a sense of pride a man
carries. Veterans come up to Victor and tell him they know
he's a vet by the way he holds himself. Chest out, head high.
It's always in the back of his mind that he served, that he
did something special. He knows his father felt the same
way. He taught Victor to walk with pride. He taught him
how to march and play soldier when Victor was a kid. He
taught him how to shoot, how to build a fire, cut a tree, find
food, water, shelter. He always treated Victor like a man. He
was father, teacher, and best friend. His father wasn't there
much but the little bit that he was left a big impression.

Victor says he had an off-and-on childhood because of his parents' divorce. But the time he spent with his father was always good. Victor never asked his father about his divorce from his mother. His parents seemed to get together and then split up every other day. Loving, fighting, loving, fighting. His father would leave and come back, leave and come back. But he never just disappeared. He'd be around. He'd call.

"You're taught in the military that if you're involved in a domestic dispute, the safe bet is to leave," Victor says. "It may not be the right decision, but it prevents you from getting in trouble."

His father would get in trouble a little bit with the police because of drinking. Victor grew used to it. He kept his mouth shut, looked the other way Whatever his father did, Victor didn't want those things to ruin his idea of who his father really was: the cool, laid-back man who loved to barbecue. From Victor's point of view, his father was an adult. He knew what to do and what not to do. He was a grown man. He didn't need a young guy to tell him how to behave.

His father was never down, no matter his problems. He was always upbeat, smiling and fun to be around. The day before Victor left for boot camp, they barbecued together. His father and mother were not together then.

Victor was infuriated when his father was deported. To do that to a vet. Send him to jail, OK, but don't deport him. Like spitting on his service. He earned his citizenship. Victor wonders if he should trust the government. What keeps it from sending him to Mexico?

His father called him from Juarez, and they talked a little here and there. He was the same guy. Telling Victor to take care. Be careful.

"You be careful," Victor said. "I got Marines watching me. You're by yourself."

"I can handle myself," his father said.

That was the kind of person he was, Victor says. His father told him stories. Fourteen people shot in Juarez. Body parts thrown out of a car to warn witnesses to be quiet. Those kind of stories.

He knew his father was a little sick, but he didn't pry. When his father died, Victor's brother called and told him. He took an emergency leave and drove home from Camp Pendleton, a good little drive from there to El Paso, you bet, he says.

After the church service, a hearse carried his father to Fort Bliss. Four soldiers carried the coffin. They presented the flag to Victor's grandmother. She gave it to Victor. The soldiers fired a twenty-one-gun salute and lowered the coffin into the ground. They played "Taps." The music reminded Victor he had lost quite a few Marines.

He has not visited the grave since.

When Luis Ortiz talks of his uncle Manny these days, he thinks of a 21-year-old Army soldier from Lebanon. The soldier has his residency card. When he was in basic training, no one helped him get his citizenship. He has a computer degree. He's a good kid. Luis helped him apply for citizenship. Luis has friends in the military from Peru, the Dominican Republic. They are all legal residents. He has seen how they've been treated. How some of the guys put them down, give them the short end of the stick. KP duty. They didn't join to do that. Once the Lebanese kid passes his citizenship test, he'll take the oath in front of the whole command. Luis feels his uncle should have been allowed to take the oath too. He wore the same uniform as everyone else.

On my last day in El Paso, Clavo and I stand among the graves at Fort Bliss and look down at Castano's white marble tombstone.

Manuel De Jesus Castano
    Spc 4
    U.S. Army
    October 1, 1957
    June 14, 2012
    Beloved father, son and brother

Clavo had also attended the funeral Mass. He felt very sad. Only a few people other than the immediate family attended. Clavo invited other vets but none of them showed up.

We look at the two tombstones on either side of Castano.

Reynaldo Garcia.
U.S. Army, Vietnam.
Beloved husband, father, brother and son.

Jose Luis Alarcon.
USAF.
Loving husband, father and grandfather.

Clavo raises his gaze beyond these two graves to the many others standing in line, one after another. A stark blue sky domes the cemetery. Brown gravel absorbs the sun. Tree branches sway, casting lean shadows over small flags and plastic flowers. A woman stands off in the distance, staring at a tombstone.

Watching her, Clavo imagines all the stories held here never to be told. He thinks of his own story. He screwed up in ways similar to Castano. He drank. But he was fortunate. He didn't get picked up by the police. But even if he had been stopped, charged, and convicted of the same crimes that put Castano in jail, he wouldn't have been deported. He cannot help but feel how privileged he is. His family moved to the

U.S. from Mexico. He was born in New Mexico. He has a U.S. birth certificate. He has the rights that come with it. Life is different for him than for so many others because he can say, I'm a citizen. That saved him.

He imagines Castano enlisting in the Army. A young man in his dress uniform on the parade ground, a future before him as bright as the light glinting off the stands. Clavo assumes Castano probably felt like a citizen too, patriotic and gung-ho, but some big shot thought differently. Well, that was then.

"You're home now, brother," Clavo says.

After Ashley

Gray, low skies hover above us, and a blustery wind cools the late August afternoon in Fairview Park Cemetery. The woman beside me, Olivia Segura, imagines her daughter Ashley in the grave at her feet. Her bones so cold. Ashley never liked the cold. Cold weather made her legs ache, even as a girl. Olivia supposes she is OK now. That where she is she does not feel cold.

The wind tugs at Olivia's dark hair, tied loosely into a fraying ponytail. Her baggy, black striped sweatshirt flaps against her body. Olivia is 48. She is not tall and neither am I, and the expanse of graves unfolding around us, with their huge black tombstones, makes the two of us smaller and renders us more insignificant among so many absent.

Olivia's daughter lies beneath a trim marble tombstone with her name, (Ashley Sietsema), the date of her birth (September 1987) and death (November 12, 2007), her rank in the Illinois Army Reserves (Army health care specialist and ambulance driver, 708th Medical Company) and where she served (Persian Gulf).

I saw photos of Ashley in newspaper clips online. She was wearing her green uniform. Her short hair was combed back behind her ears. A broad grin opened her face, her eyes alight and smiling.

Ashley died in a car accident while conducting a routine medical transfer of a patient from Camp Buehring to Camp Arifjan in Kuwait. Her family fell apart. Her stepfather, Alberto Segura, tried to drink his grief away. Her brother Kyle locked himself in his room. Her mother doped herself with sleeping pills.

It took another crisis, the 2009 arrest of Alberto, an undocumented immigrant, to pull the family together. Olivia and Kyle successfully worked for his release. Afterward, Olivia returned to college and earned a bachelor of arts. She formed the Ashley Project to champion families of veterans killed in the line of duty. Among other things, she began advocating for deported veterans. Kyle graduated from high school and began working to help support the family and save money for college.

Alberto, however, had few options. He was free but unable to work because of a prior felony drug conviction, and repeated arrests for driving under the influence made him ineligible for citizenship. Olivia and Kyle moved forward. Alberto stayed behind.

"We were happy but stressed," Olivia said. "It was too hard for me to be the main provider. I'm not a lazy person, but I was not meant to be the main provider. I was with Alberto but alone because he couldn't contribute."

Something had to give. Eventually, something did. Alberto began drinking again, and the family collapsed once more. Not the same way as before, although there was certainly drama, but in the small bruises collected on the way down, refracting all the now familiar anguish that had followed Ashley's death and had never been fully reconciled.

I heard about Alberto and Olivia from Cesar Lopez, the deported Marine who crossed back into the U.S. He had met Olivia on the deported veterans Facebook page. I became intrigued by Alberto's story. It was different from the other deported veteran stories I had covered. This time, a veteran wasn't the one without papers but the vet's stepfather.

I looked up the Seguras on Facebook. A photo of Alberto showed a large, 46-year-old man with a thick head of black hair combed back off his forehead. He had a smile that filled the photo. I called the Seguras and spoke to Alberto in July 2016. He was soft-spoken but eager to discuss his situation. We agreed to talk again at the end of the month to arrange a meeting.

Two weeks later, I reached Olivia instead of Alberto. She told me police had arrested him for driving under the influence. He was facing four to fifteen years in jail. Olivia didn't know if his case would be flagged by federal authorities for removal proceedings and referred to immigration court.

His drinking made her furious but the possibility of his deportation angered her more. Punish him, yes. Get him help, yes.

"But deport?" she said. "No. Ashley died for this country. That should mean something."

Here in the cemetery, her anger has been weakened by uncertainty.

"I don't know what will happen," she says.

She speaks to Ashley, tells her what's going on. She assumes Ashley knows. In death, Ashley has become her guardian angel, Olivia says. She promises Ashley she will help Alberto. Ashley had no relationship with her biological father, who abandoned her and Olivia when Ashley was a toddler. Alberto was the only father she knew. She called him by his name but they were very close. She was daddy's girl.

Olivia shakes her head and lets out a long breath. Alberto is stuck. He has boxed himself into a corner. She doesn't know how to get him out and get on with her life, too. She misses Ashley and struggles these many years later to cope with her grief. Olivia needs to end this. She can't take any more crises, any more pain. She feels as if she has failed somehow. She believes in marriage. In sickness and in health, through good times and bad. A husband shouldn't be left alone. They deserve a full commitment. But she feels she has given everything she has to Alberto. Since Ashley died, she has borne an incredible weight. She wants to shed that weight. "I'm going to leave him," Olivia tells me. "I'm tired of living like this."

Repeating her vow to Ashley, Olivia says she will help Alberto once more. Beyond that, she won't promise.

Kyle Segura sits across from me in the breakfast nook of the Segura house. Ashley had painted the walls orange and yellow. Three mixed-breed dogs of varying sizes scramble around our feet rocking the table, their nails clackety-clacking against the hardwood floor. Kyle wears black glasses. He folds his hands on the table and looks at me intently. I ask him questions and he considers his words for moments at a time before he speaks. Then he talks in a calm, measured way without hesitation. He tells me he visits the cemetery from time to time. Not as much as his mother but every now and then.

He was thirteen when Ashley died. Her death made him grow up real fast. He gets along better with people older than him than he does friends his own age. He is twenty-two but thinks like a thirty-year-old, he says. He should be partying but he can't because his forty-year-old dad did and is now in jail.

"I'd be a really strict judge," Kyle says.

He doesn't want to see his father deported but if he were a judge he'd throw the book at him. Kyle feels a fury that competes with his love for his father. He gets it, his father got stressed out again. But if drinking put him in jail before, why do it again? Hit a punching bag to get your frustrations out. "Do you see why I don't hang out with people my own age?" Kyle asks me. "How can they understand? How can anyone?"

Kyle's voice remains steady, his anger dialed back almost immediately to a controlled simmer. He objected to his mother's decision to help his father. Not this time. How could they afford a lawyer? Kyle has a factory job and gets to work at 5 a.m. He helps his mother pay the mortgage. He should be in college, but instead he has to do this because his father could not work, drank, and is now in jail.

Sometimes he starts toward Ashley's bedroom to talk to her about it. Then he stops himself. Oh, wait you're not here. Kyle has experienced other losses: a friend died of cancer and another friend—his closest—killed himself. When he skateboards, he thinks, Look what I am doing, dude. You see this? And then it's like, Oh, he's dead, too.

He hates this. The loss. The emptiness. He feels that the closer he gets to people, the worse their lives will be. He spends a loft of time alone. Like his mother, Kyle speaks to Ashley when he visits her grave. He says, I miss you. I don't know what to do. Give me a sign. She probably does, but Kyle doesn't see it. That sucks.

Olivia grew up in Unidad Rosario, a neighborhood of Mexico City. Her white house had a living room, kitchen, dining room, and a patio. Three bedrooms took up the second floor. A one-car garage stood attached to the house.

Olivia was the oldest of three girls. She remembers her father taking her skydiving. She did it to please him. He had wanted boys, not girls. He always brought this up with Olivia's mother. Oh, yeah, you didn't give me boys. He wanted his girls to be tough. He was so proud of her when she jumped. She liked the speed, the rush just before the chute opened, and then the calm of floating in air as she maneuvered the chute. She jumped about eleven times before she broke her right leg. She was in a cast for three months and never jumped again. These days, she doesn't like taking risks. Life is too important, she explains.

Her father, an electrician, also volunteered with the Red Cross and would take Olivia with him. She would see all these people from around the world who worked with him. They spoke about other countries they had worked in. She wanted to be like them. Well-traveled, worldly, and learned.

In 1985, her father's brother-in-law offered him a position at a Chicago tire company and he accepted. He told his family they would move to the United States for five years so he could earn enough money to send his daughters to college.

Olivia, fifteen at the time, had no desire to leave Mexico. She didn't speak English. She knew no one in Chicago. She asked to stay in Mexico City with her grandmother but her father refused. He didn't think Olivia's grandmother was strong enough to supervise a rebellious teenager. In those days, children were raised not to talk back to their parents, but Olivia was opinionated. She questioned everything.

Equipped with visitor visas, the family moved to Chicago in February. They lived with an aunt on the North Side. But they wanted their own place so they didn't feel like guests. Olivia's father rented a one-bedroom basement apartment. It was not like their Mexico home. Olivia's mother turned the pantry into a second bedroom so they'd all have a place to sleep. Olivia missed having her own room and hanging out with her friends. She made new ones at Wells High School, but she had no time to hang out with them because her father pushed her to find a job. She found part-time work in a small clinic and earned $40 a week. She turned her meager salary over to her mother.

In 1986, Olivia was walking past a basketball court on Milwaukee Avenue, when a young man called her over. He was also from Mexico, and they got to talking. They had been dating for about a year when, in March 1987, Olivia became pregnant. They decided to marry. Olivia's father escorted her down the aisle. He told her her husband was no good. Walk away, he said. But she refused. She was in love. Her father didn't talk to her for six months.

Ashley was born in September. The marriage did not last. In 1990, Olivia's husband left her for another woman. Her family had moved back to Mexico, so Olivia took Ashley to live there for a while, but she did not stay long. She had become a legal U.S. resident. Chicago was home now. She held out the hope that she and her husband would get back together. She returned to Chicago and saw him a few times but he did not want to be with her.

Olivia met Alberto in 1992 at Morton College in Chicago. The two of them had agreed to help move a mutual acquaintance. Alberto had on jeans and a T-shirt. At first, Olivia didn't like him. He was always looking at her. Why aren't you picking up the sofa and taking it through this door? he asked her. Because, stupid, she said, it won't fit. He laughed and after a while she could not help but laugh, too. Later, they shared a pizza.

Olivia told Alberto about her failed marriage. He talked about his family. He was born in Mexico and had four brothers and a sister. His father died when he was eight, and he dropped out of school to work and support the family. He sold ice cream. He worked in the public markets. He walked to the garbage dumps and sold what he found, discarded clothes, shoes, anything. His mother never remarried. She did not want to risk taking on a man who might be abusive to children not his own. She and Alberto's brothers worked, too, and Alberto rarely saw them. In high school, he worked in a slaughterhouse. He told Olivia how he carried large slabs of beef over his shoulders throughout the day.

Alberto married at eighteen but his wife died in childbirth. She was an only child, and his mother-in-law blamed him for her death. Alberto drank a lot after the loss of his wife and traveled aimlessly around Mexico. He had a brother in Chicago. At loose ends and still grieving, he left his baby with his in-laws and moved to the States in 1989.

Olivia and Alberto began dating. He was very nice, she says. He'd buy presents for Ashley. He worked in shipping and receiving and helped Olivia with money. She wonders now if she was in love or just kind of. Was she just lonely?

They were not yet married when she became pregnant with Kyle. Olivia thought, I'm not ready to have another baby. She worried the baby would not have a future and decided to have an abortion but Alberto stopped her. He met her outside the clinic. That is my son, he told her. I won't have any son or daughter of mine killed. He assured Olivia everything would work out. The baby would have a future. He would provide. Olivia relented. She let Alberto take charge. Kyle was born in 1994.

Kyle remembers the days his father would come home from whatever construction job he had, just some random day, and say, C'mon, we're going on vacation. He waved away any argument from Kyle's mother. New York City, Disneyland, the amusement park in Cedar Point, Ohio. Kyle loved these breaks. It was sweet to cut out of school for a few days. He'd grab his video game bag and was the first one ready to leave.

Kyle didn't think of Ashley as a stepsister. Looking back, he thinks she didn't care for him all that much at first. Seven years separated them. He had that annoying little brother thing going on. He wanted to hang with her and her older friends. His mother and father were always working, so she had little choice but to watch him. When Kyle was a kid, Ashley worked at Jeepers!, a Chuck E Cheese sort of place. He accompanied her to work and she gave him tokens for arcade games.

As he got older, Ashley told him to get involved in sports. She liked basketball, hockey, skateboarding. Kyle liked skateboarding but thought hockey was too violent.

Alberto didn't treat her like a stepdaughter, Kyle recalls. They were close. When Kyle wanted to do something, he asked his mother, but Ashley would always ask Alberto. Sometimes Kyle did, too. When he got in trouble at school for not doing his homework, he called his father. So this is what happened, he would say to Alberto. Would you tell the teacher it's not my fault? OK, Alberto said. No trouble. You can make it up. Don't do it again.

His father was laid-back. In those days, Kyle never saw him drink.

In 1997, Alberto and Olivia married. They left Chicago and bought a house in Melrose Park, a suburb. Olivia hoped to go back to school but the need to work and support two children took precedence. Alberto always had a job in those days. Yard work, construction, something. He did his part, Olivia says.

He used to drink casually at parties. Nothing to cause Olivia concern. He never got into trouble until 2004 when Maywood police pulled him over for driving under the influence. They also found $20 worth of cocaine in his possession. Olivia found out about the coke when she attended his trial. Alberto had said he had been busted for drinking only. He hadn't mentioned drugs. Afterward he told her he had hung out with the wrong kind of people at a construction job. Try this, they told him. He did, and he liked it.

Alberto pled guilty. He was sentenced to six months of house arrest and wore an electronic ankle bracelet. Olivia's disappointment turned to mistrust. She held all their cash, including his paychecks and credit cards. She put gas in their cars herself so he would have no need to handle money for even the slightest task. She maintained tight control over their lives until Ashley died. Alberto didn't object, Olivia says, but he didn't like it. It's like you're watching me all the time, he told her.

Despite the tension in their marriage, the Seguras continued as a family. Every Friday the four of them drove to the mall to select videos to rent for the weekend. They'd usually pick four movies and then stop and order Chinese food.

In 2001, after the 9/11 terrorist attacks, Ashley enrolled in her high school's ROTC program. Three years later she asked her parents if she could enlist in the Illinois National

Guard. Since she was only 16, she needed parental approval. Olivia refused to give it. Why join the Guard? We can send you to college, she told her daughter. You don't need the extra money.

Ashley wanted to be a nurse and perhaps later study to be a doctor. The Guard's medical corps would give her great experience, she'd said. Ashley always wanted to help people, Olivia says. She taught Bible study to kids at Sunday school, and she was like a mother to Kyle. She was very mature. Olivia thought she would make a great nurse, a great doctor. But she still did not want her to join the Guard.

Alberto, however, supported Ashley. Olivia argued with him but Alberto would not back down. We need to support her, he said. She'll do it anyway when she's eighteen. We are here to support our daughter. We don't want to make a decision now we'll regret later. Olivia relented. Ashley joined the Guard in 2004.

After she graduated from high school, Ashley enrolled in Northern Illinois University in DeKalb, Illinois. The Seguras decided to move to the university town so the family could stay together. Ashley picked the house, a two-story home in a cul-de-sac. A large living room overlooked a fenced backyard. When Alberto and Olivia retired, they told Ashley, they would leave the house to her.

In March 2007 and three months before her deployment, Ashley married Max Sietsema, whom she had dated in high school. Olivia opposed the marriage. She did not want Ashley to make the same mistakes she had and have children before she established a career. She thought Ashley, nineteen at the time, was too young. She should finish college first. But Alberto insisted they both attend the wedding.

You'll regret it for the rest of your life if you don't, he told her.

Kyle hated to leave Melrose Park for DeKalb. DeKalb was a backward little town out of a horror movie, he thought. The house Ashley liked reminded him of a library. Ashley bribed him. She promised to give him a video game, Pokédex from Pokémon, if he promised not to create a fuss. Kyle agreed. I'll bring the game, Ashley said. Kyle was eleven or twelve at the time.

He remembers the night she first spoke to their parents about joining the Guard. They were finishing dinner. Ashley assured their mother, I'll be a medic. I won't go to war. I won't be on the front line. Kyle didn't think much of it. Maybe he was too young to understand, he says now. He was just a kid. He looked at it like she was taking a vacation. She'd be gone and then she'd be back by Thanksgiving maybe, Christmas for sure. And their lives would resume like she had never left.

His mother's face paled as Ashley talked about going to Kuwait. Casual. Like she was wondering aloud what she'd have for dessert. Kyle assumes now that deep inside her nerves were wound tight. Whose wouldn't be? But she held her chin up. Proud, calm, ready. Alberto said nothing. Kyle's mother turned to him but he avoided her look.

The Seguras would drop Ashley off for training in North Lake, Illinois, on weekends. Kyle saw the barracks and the people running exercises. He thought the Guard looked pretty cool.

Ashley would talk about the training when she came home. She told him about all the exercises they had to do. Climbing over walls, all the running. She got into it. She liked challenges. Sometimes she was so tired Kyle had a hard time understanding her.

Ashley became more demanding of herself after she enlisted with the Guard, Kyle says. Stricter. She would still laugh and joke and be laid back but she took on more of a leadership role in the house. She would cook dinner for Kyle and not wait for their parents to come home from work.

Kyle liked her husband, Max. Max became an older brother to him. In the summer, he'd invite Kyle along to Taste of Chicago, a weekend-long outdoor jamboree of some of the city's best restaurants.

Hey, what do you think if me and Max get married? Ashley asked him.

Cool, Kyle said.

Kyle knew his mother didn't approve but his father did. His father was always very supportive, very proud of Ashley.

When Ashley deployed, Kyle asked her not to go. Why can't you stay home, go to school, get married, get pregnant, and call it quits?

If everyone stayed home and got pregnant we would not be a free country, she told him.

Ashley left for Kuwait on June 15, 2007. Olivia had lunch with her the day before at an Olive Garden restaurant. On the way, she stopped to buy Ashley two blouses as a going-away gift, and she was late. Ashley looked annoyed. She hated tardiness. She was always fifteen minutes early to everything.

"You're late," she said.

"Here's your present. For over there since you can't be here for your birthday."

Ashley smiled then and hugged Olivia.

"It's OK you're late this time," she said.

Ashley called weekly from Kuwait. She said how different everything was there. How women wore clothes that covered their faces and bodies. How the people prayed at certain times of the day. Sometimes, Ashley had to get off the phone so she would not be talking while people attended mosque. She liked the food. The most popular dish was "Machboos," chicken, beef or fish over a specially spiced rice. The weather was something else, Ashley said. Very hot.

On the morning of November 11, 2007, Olivia and Alberto got up as usual and made breakfast. They sat together at the kitchen table. The day was cold but sunny.

"Oh, my God," Olivia said. "Christmas is coming soon. I can't wait to see what Ashley brings me."

"Instead of waiting, you should worry about her coming home safe," Alberto snapped. ("For no reason," Olivia says now. "Like he sensed something.")

"Stupid gifts," he shouted.

"Yes, you're right," Olivia said, and dropped the subject.

They said nothing further and finished their coffee. Olivia went to the supermarket. She was putting groceries away when she heard someone knocking. She opened the front door and two Army Reserve officers introduced themselves. One of them asked if she had any health problems. Bad heart? Blood pressure?

"No," Olivia said. "Is this about Ashley? Did she get in an accident?"

"You need to sit down."

Olivia shouted for Alberto.

"She did have an accident," one of the officers said. "We're here to notify you. She died. We don't have any more details."

Olivia started shaking. Then she got angry. She threw a vase filled with flowers. She broke down in tears. She doesn't remember what Alberto was doing.

"I want my daughter back!" she cried.

A week later, Ashley's body arrived at DeKalb Taylor Municipal Airport. Men and women holding flags lined the streets of DeKalb as the hearse passed. More people Olivia did not know filled the church, including the governor.

Ashley was the second Illinois reservist to die in the Iraq War that year.

In the days that followed Ashley's funeral, Olivia took pills to sleep and Alberto drank. Olivia stayed in bed days on end. She had dreams. Ashley would come to her and ask about Max, her husband. He is OK, Olivia told her. Did soldiers come to the house from the Guard? Yes, Olivia told her. She told Ashley to follow the light.

When Olivia awoke, she cried. She felt an inconsolable grief. She felt like she was dying. She took more pills and slept again.

Olivia blamed Alberto for Ashley's death. It's your fault, she told him. You made me sign the enlistment papers. Why did you allow her to enlist? Olivia wanted to destroy Alberto. You're a killer, she said. She hit him, slapped him. He never struck back, she says.

She and Alberto stopped talking to one another. Every time a car came by the house they would watch it pass, hoping it might turn into their driveway. Maybe it would be the Army coming to tell them that they had made a mistake.

One afternoon, Olivia stopped at a Wal-Mart and the cashier asked her, Do you have children? Yes, Olivia said. A daughter. She's studying to be a nurse and then a doctor. When she got home, she broke down.

Kyle remembers accompanying his parents to O'Hare Airport in June 2007 to drop off Ashley for her deployment. He saw so many soldiers, men and women. He thought, Man, this is serious.

During Ashley's deployment, Kyle got in trouble at school for being late. His mom grounded him. She also told Ashley. What's going through your head, Kyle? Ashley chided him in an email. I know how hard it is to deal with school and mom but don't back talk. Do well. Get out there. Go to college. It's a tough world. Use your mind.

Ashley would call him from Kuwait on Skype. She'd ask him what he was up to. Nothing much, he'd say. Probably watch the Bears game. He was taking guitar lessons and he jammed some punk music he learned from a Blink 182 album for her. Ashley told him she couldn't wait to be home for Christmas.

Kyle's aunt was visiting the morning the two Army reservists came to the house. Kyle was running late to class as usual. He didn't hear what the soldiers said but he heard his mother shout, Not my daughter! and then he saw her drop to the floor. Kyle's aunt grabbed him. I'm so sorry, she told him. Kyle didn't understand. He said, Please tell me nothing bad happened. Why's mom crying?

His father tried to hold Kyle's mother, but he was crying, too. The soldiers stayed about an hour trying to calm them. His father sent Kyle to his room. This is a rough time, we have to be strong, his father told him. It's OK to cry. No one told him directly but he knew Ashley had died. He didn't understand how he should feel. He had not known anyone who had died.

Kyle stayed in his room. So many people began dropping by the house. He hated it. He had no desire to see anyone. He didn't attend school for a week. At the Ronan-Moore-Finch Funeral home, he saw the open casket, Ashley's body wrapped in white. People approached Kyle. Sorry for your loss. The same thing over and over again. Sorry for your loss. Sorry for your loss.

At the church service, the priest asked if anyone wanted to say a few words. Kyle wanted to get up but couldn't. He was so angry. He wanted to say, You all know Ashley. We lost an amazing person. She always put others before herself. She was my best friend. A mother to me, too. He wanted to say how much her death sucked.

Kyle returned to school a week later. He didn't speak to anyone. He didn't want to be there. He didn't want to be home, either. His mother would be doped up on sleeping pills, his father drunk. He tried to keep his mind busy, do things like ice skating. He would stay out late. Sometimes, he wouldn't come home before nine or ten at night. His parents didn't acknowledge him. No one cooked. Kyle retreated to his room, forgotten.

One January afternoon in 2009, Kyle came home from school. His father sat drunk on the couch. Kyle flipped out. Ashley had been dead more than two years and he was just tired of being treated as if he didn't exist, as if he had died, too.

"I'm here," he shouted at his father. "I'm sick of being ignored. You and mom don't care. You only think of Ashley. If you want to drink, go to a bar. You might as well leave."

His father didn't say anything, Kyle says. He took it all in and then stood up and walked out. Kyle blames himself for his arrest. If he hadn't mouthed off, none of that would have happened.

Alberto had been piling up the DUIs. Three in March 2008 alone. He got into fights at work and lost a landscaping job. On that January day when Alberto argued with Kyle and left the house, he didn't come back. Olivia thought he had left her. She no longer cared. She didn't ask about him, didn't look for him.

But her situation and depression continued to worsen. A short time after his arrest, Olivia had gallbladder surgery, brought on, she said, by stress. Then Kyle suffered appendicitis. Olivia's health insurance did not cover all the medical costs and she sunk deeply into debt. What more can happen?

Her despondency reached a point where she considered suicide by giving herself and Kyle a lethal amount of her sleeping pills.

"Do you want to sleep forever?" she asked Kyle one night.
They sat in the living room on a brown leather couch so
worn Olivia covered it with a blanket to conceal the holes.
The evening sky had darkened to tar and lights from houses shined in isolated patches. And Olivia could hear traffic
outside, distant and vague until she heard nothing at all but
the sound of her own voice.

"Do you want us to die?" he asked her.

The bluntness of the question stopped her. She had just
reached a point where she wanted to be happy again and not
always feeling awful, but she did not want to die.

"No, no," she said. "Go to bed and we'll wake up tomorrow."

In March 2009, she received a call from the wife of an
inmate at Cook County Jail. She told Olivia she got her name
from her husband, who knew Alberto.

"Your husband's in prison," she told Olivia. "He's depressed. He wants to end his life."

Olivia began crying.

"You don't know what he's done. It is his fault my daughter died."

"I'm sorry you feel that way," the woman said. "But you
have to take some responsibility. You can't go on fighting all
the time. I know from my husband that he loves you and
your son."

Olivia visited Alberto the next day. He told her he had left
the house and driven into Chicago. He had nowhere to stay.
He parked the car and slept on the street. He had a bottle of
vodka. He had not shut off the ignition and police saw the
car running and took him in.

Alberto's plight brought Olivia back to life. No one is separating my family, she tells me she thought at the time. They
took my daughter. They won't take my husband.

She hired a lawyer. She wrote to politicians and explained
Ashley's death and how it had affected the family. When
someone joins the military, we all join, she wrote. We can't
sleep. We worry. When they die, we die with them.

She also prayed to Ashley. Why did you leave me? she
asked her daughter. Do you know how painful this is? I wish
you hadn't joined the military. I'll make a deal with you. I'll
never ask you why you didn't come home again. I'll forgive
you. All I'm asking you now is to please bring your father
home.

Kyle noticed a change come over his mother. She stopped
taking sleeping pills. She told Kyle she'd take care of the situation. She'd visit his father in prison. You stay here, she
said. Clean the house. She left, and he wondered if she would
come back.

When she returned home hours later, Olivia told Kyle,
This is what we'll do. I need you to do this. She gave him
a list. Get supportive letters for your father, look around
the house for anything that shows how long he has been in
Illinois. Find photos of the family. Find papers documenting
Ashley's service.

Kyle did what she asked. She didn't say anything about
not being there for him after Ashley died. That bothered
him. But it felt good to see his mother back to normal. He
had had no mother for more than a year.

"Your father will come home," she told him.

Alberto served a year in prison. On January 5, 2010, after
he completed his sentence, he was transferred to McHenry
County Adult Correctional Facility, an Immigration and
Customs Enforcement facility. Immigration Judge Craig M.

Zerbe closed the case without deporting Alberto six days later "for humanitarian considerations" because of Ashley's death. However, Alberto's release did not resolve his status. He remained undocumented. At the time of his release, employers had access to E-Verify, an internet-based system that allows businesses to determine the eligibility of their employees to work in the States. Alberto would no longer be able to find work unless it was under the table.

The family fell behind. When Alberto did find a job, every dime went into delinquent bills. And then the employer would find out Alberto was not a citizen and fire him. Alberto tried to make jewelry to earn money. He sold a little but not much. He was always chasing something. The Seguras were always trying to catch up. Desperate, Alberto and Olivia sought a pardon from then-Governor Pat Quinn for Alberto's drug conviction and DUIs. Friends and some politicians wrote letters on his behalf. They heard nothing.

"I can't support the family by myself," Olivia told Alberto.

"What else can I do?" he would say. "I'm not getting a job without this pardon. I feel useless no matter what I try to do."

"As long as you don't drink, you'll be OK," Olivia told him.

Olivia continued to dream about Ashley. In one, she recalled a conversation they had in 2006 a year before she deployed.

"Why don't you finish college?" Ashley had asked her.

"Why? Because I can't afford it."

"You gave me everything and put yourself in second place."

"Do you think I'm smart enough to go back to school now?"

"You can do anything you want."

"Well, it will have to wait."

"When I become a doctor, I'll pay for you to go to the university."

When she woke up, Olivia asked herself, What am I doing with my life? I need to do something for Ashley.

She enrolled in DeVry University in Chicago and graduated in 2012 with a degree in information technology.

Despite the pressures of work and school, Olivia continued to advocate for Alberto. In 2015, she met the recently elected Illinois governor, Bruce Rauner, at a prayer breakfast for Gold Star mothers. He gave a short talk and then moved among the tables. Olivia told him about Alberto and gave him a letter requesting a pardon. The governor, she says, smiled and said he'd do what he could. He gave her letter to an aide.

A year later, in June 2016, Alberto's request for a pardon was denied. He started drinking. Little by little, not every day, Olivia says. They began seeing a priest every Friday for couples counseling. The priest suggested Alberto attend meetings of Alcoholics Anonymous.

Olivia stayed active. She became involved with deported veterans after her pastor told her about the issue. When they are removed, their families are left behind the same as if they had died, her pastor said.

In July 2016, Olivia flew to San Diego and crossed the border into Tijuana for a rally on behalf of deported veterans. She held a sign: Stop deporting veterans. She met with Hector Barajas-Varela. She told him about Ashley. When a veteran goes through a hard time it is my hard time, she said, because Ashley was a veteran. Ashley believed in the slogan "No Man Left Behind." Olivia thought someone should say no families left behind, too. She said her husband, the stepfather of a veteran, needed help. He should be given a chance on behalf of his daughter's service. He should be allowed to become a citizen.

While she was away, Alberto lost a factory job. He had lied to get it. He said he was in the process of getting his paperwork. When it didn't come through, he was fired. He had hoped to work there a long time. Olivia noticed he was upset when she spoke to him by phone but he would not say why. He did not pick her up at Midway Airport like he had promised when she returned to Chicago. He was not in the house when she finally made it home after paying a cab driver $200 for the two-hour drive from the airport to DeKalb. The next morning, she learned he had been arrested for drunken driving.

When his father didn't come home, Kyle suspected the worst. He checked county jails online. What's between DeKalb and Chicago? he asked himself. Kane County. He clicked on the county's web page and typed his father's name.

Shit, I don't want to do this again, Kyle said to himself when his father's name came up. We're just getting out of debt. I don't want to do this whole save-my-dad thing again.

Kyle has visited his father in jail. He talked to him on the phone, too. His father has apologized to him. He told Kyle he understood if Olivia wanted to leave him. This time, he said, he wanted to quit drinking. He didn't want to end up alone, dying alone. As much as Kyle wants to be angry with him, he can't. His father is his father but Kyle doesn't quite know what to do. Maybe jail would be good for him. Maybe he would get the help he needs.

Kyle wishes Ashley were here. He would tell her, if you were alive none of this would be happening. But she's not here so what's the point? He wishes she would see him graduate college. See him get married when the time comes if it does. But she won't be here. Sucks.

A reservist came by the house one time, Kyle says. A guy named Velez. He found Kyle on Myspace. I was in Ashley's unit, he wrote. Can I meet you guys? He and his wife and child drove over. He gave the family $500 to help them out. He said he would always be there for them. He broke down. He blamed himself. He should have been the one driving, he said, but he was tired. Oh, let me drive, Ashley told him. She died right away. She didn't suffer. He closed her eyes and that was that. He started shaking and crying louder. He hugged Kyle's mother. He asked forgiveness.

"Don't blame yourself," she told him.

"I blame myself," he said.

Kyle held him.

"Things happen because they do," he said.

He never heard from Velez again.

Max also fell out of touch. He came by once in 2008 to pick up a car Ashley owned. He didn't want to see Kyle's mother. She reminded him too much of Ashley. Kyle has not seen him since.

Olivia visits Alberto in jail for the thirty minutes allowed. They look at each other, divided by glass. It's like seeing him through a computer, she says. He has told her he doesn't know why he does what he does. He recognizes he made a mistake. He says he knows he has an alcohol problem. The police report said he took a breathalyzer test. He was four times over the legal limit. He yelled, Fuck off, puto, at the police when they arrested him. I'll kill you when I get out, he said.

His lawyer read the police report. He told Olivia he did not know how much help he could provide. The breathalyzer results hurt his case. Swearing and threatening police officers hurts his case. Being undocumented hurts his case.

Worst-case scenario he could be sentenced to four to fifteen years in jail. He might also be deported.

Alberto asked Olivia to move to Mexico should he be removed from the country. She told him she would not do that. This is my country now, she said. I've been here since I was fifteen. My life is here. Kyle is here. Ashley is here. I can't leave her behind.

Kyle hopes his father doesn't face deportation again. He hopes he gets out of prison in a couple of years. This is all about saving him from himself, Kyle says. If he doesn't get deported, it would be such a huge relief.

These days, he feels OK around his mother. It wasn't long ago when Kyle would have said, Hell no, I don't want to be around her. She doesn't care about me. He says he understands now that she was not ignoring him. She just didn't know how to deal with Ashley's death. He doesn't blame her. God forbid, should the same thing happen to him, he wouldn't know how to cope with the loss of a child either. His mother looks at him from time to time and says I'm sorry. Sorry for everything.

It's OK, Kyle tells her. He asks nothing from her. He has forgiven her. He has forgiven his father, too, and Ashley for leaving them.

Kyle hopes to attend college. He wants to minor in film and major in law. He doesn't want to waste time. Ashley never did. She was always productive. But look what happened to her. Kyle doesn't know what life holds. He could die at any time. His mother and father could, too. He might be left alone again.

In the cemetery, grass rustles at the base of Ashley's tombstone, stirred by the wind. Sparrows rise and fall in its currents and larger birds take shelter in trees. Olivia stands with her hands in her pockets. She tells Ashley about an undocumented Iraq War veteran facing deportation. Special Forces. Came home, got in trouble with drugs and was sentenced to prison. As soon as he is released he will be moved to an immigration detention center. He has post-traumatic stress disorder. Olivia has become his advocate.

She also has a new job with Nestle. Clerical work. Fourteen dollars an hour. Not as much as she'd like. She is not guaranteed forty hours a week. She doesn't get sick days, holidays. She has a bachelor of arts. Someone with her skills should do better, she says. Maybe it's her Mexican accent that holds her back, she tells Ashley. Maybe her age. Maybe because she's a woman.

Olivia worries about Kyle. She demands a lot from him. She needs him to help pay the bills. She needs him to hang out with her. She hates to be alone. She needs him as a son and so much more. She asks a lot of him. She feels she has failed him.

"We don't like to talk about Ashley, do we?" she said to him one afternoon.

"You don't, Mom," he said.

She often thinks about that afternoon and what Kyle told her. You don't, Mom. Olivia has yet to adjust to life without her daughter. She told Alberto, If we stay together we can't go back to the way it was after Ashley died.

After her daughter's death, friends stopped talking to Olivia, she tells me. She thinks now she made them uncomfortable. They didn't want to hear her sadness. She didn't chase after them. She stopped seeing her cousin. Her cousin has children. It pained Olivia to see them. It was too hard to lose a daughter and then see other families with all the things she had wanted for her children. She blames herself sometimes for her loneliness. She cut people off.

She won't cut Alberto off but she doesn't know if she'll stay with him. He has to resolve his status, Olivia says. He has to seek treatment for his alcoholism. He has to become a working part of the family again. When she remembers the good times before Ashley's death, the spur-of-the-moment vacations, the movies they watched together Friday nights, she doesn't want to leave him. He is the father of her son. He loved Ashley as his own. He is a good father.

"Ashley died for her country," Olivia says. "That should count for something."

Turning to me, she asks what I think. I shrug, shake my head, bite my lower lip, and feel a nagging doubt. She has some difficult decisions to make. I don't know if I accept her reasoning that Alberto should not be deported because he was the stepfather of a veteran. Alberto was given a break once and blew it. However, I don't see what deporting him would accomplish other than breaking up a family already coming apart. We like winners, those individuals who triumph over adversity. Losers are simply discards, especially a guy driving under the influence who is lucky he hasn't killed someone already. And there is his wife standing beside me, a fighter, resilient in her way yet lost and beaten down under burdens she can barely withstand, and who sought escape through pills and may now seek escape through divorce. The truth is that most everyone on this earth is a little of both good and bad, strong and weak, remarkable and flawed. We judge them and too often don't ask how they got that way.

Alberto has to accept responsibility but so do we. We send people to war without thinking about the consequences to the families they leave behind and the ramifications of a father or mother, son or daughter not returning home alive. After all the yellow ribbons have faded and rotted off trees

and lampposts, after all the flag waving, when their grief remains unabated, when they behave in ways that violate the
heroic, stoic images we have of a dead soldier's family, when
calling the dead "patriots" does not provide comfort, what
then do we say to those left behind?

Olivia faces the grave a moment longer. She tells Ashley
she hopes for good things. She wants her heart to jump with
joy again. She wants to move out of the shadow of her grief
and Alberto's troubles.

The wind picks up. Olivia lets out a long breath. Hunched
against the wind and the flat, gray sky bearing down. A
diminutive figure beside the grave of her daughter. If Kyle
is home, he and Olivia will eat dinner together. Maybe rent
a movie, order Chinese food. Sounds good. Like old times.

"Goodbye," she tells Ashley.

She steps slowly through the damp grass and walks alone
to her car and mulls over the evening ahead. She hopes Kyle
will be waiting for her.

Coming Home I

I return to the Bunker in September 2016, more than two years after I first met Hector Barajas-Varela. I have an appointment with Daniel Torres, a "self-deported" Iraq War vet who recently became a U.S. citizen. Torres had lied about his status to join the Marines and was thrown out of the Corp. Unable find a job in the States, he returned to Tijuana, his birthplace. None of the deported vets he knew in the Bunker had expected him to receive citizenship. Certainly not Hector Barajas-Varela, who has been trying to get home for seven years.

Barajas-Varela is sitting across from me at his cluttered desk, polishing off a plate of scrambled eggs and eyeballing messages on his Facebook page. He recalls when Torres had dropped by the support house in 2014, just another vet kicked down to Mexico because he wasn't a U.S. citizen. Torres told Barajas-Varela he'd spoken to attorneys but they offered him nothing. Typical, Barajas-Varela thought. But two years later,

191

that dour assessment has been turned on its head: Torres made it home.

Barajas-Varela himself may also return to the U.S. He has an appointment in San Diego to take the citizenship test at the end of the month. He just needs a waiver from the U.S. Embassy to enter San Diego. Barajas-Varela credits the Southern California chapter of the American Civil Liberties Union for the change in fortune for Torres and now, he hopes, for himself.

Barajas-Varela contacted the ACLU in the spring of 2015 to ask whether it would provide legal and policy support on behalf of deported veterans. He also wanted help for honorably discharged deported vets seeking to obtain their medical benefits from the U.S. Department of Veterans Affairs.

Barajas-Varela told the ACLU about the case of Jose Solorio, a deported former Marine who was dying from pulmonary fibrosis. He had been paroled by U.S. Customs and Border Protection into the country for two weeks to receive medical care.

The hospital determined a lung transplant was necessary to save Solorio's life, but he would need more than two weeks in the country for the transplant and recovery. At first, U.S. Customs and Border Protection refused to extend his parole, but reversed its decision after being contacted by the ACLU. By then it was too late. Solorio's condition had deteriorated so much that the hospital could no longer perform the transplant. He died a few days later.

Motivated in part by Solorio's death, the ACLU, with the help of Barajas-Varela and volunteers at the Bunker, contacted more than 200 deported veterans in 2015 to record their cases. The following year, volunteer attorneys from the law firm Latham & Watkins and the ACLU held a legal clinic, interviewing 59 veterans from 22 countries, all of whom had either been deported or were currently fighting deportation.*

Not all deported veterans are eligible to apply for U.S. citizenship. They can have no conviction for an aggravated felony. They also must have served during a time of war.

Torres and Barajas-Varela met the eligibility requirements. Torres had no criminal record. A change in law in 2011 found that the charge that put Barajas-Varela in prison was no longer considered an aggravated felony. He was eligible to petition for U.S. citizenship.

"It's happening pretty soon, I'm going home," Barajas-Varela says. "I'm anxious. I'm ready to go across. I'd like to get an answer the same day I take the test."

Much has changed at the Bunker since I was last here in December 2014. For one thing, the support house is empty. The vets I met on my first trip have all left, one way or another. Oscar Leyva moved out. Gonzalo Chaidez and Juan Jose Montemayor died in 2015 from tuberculosis. Alfredo "Al" Varon Guzman also died that year from complications following surgery for ascites in San Diego. He had been granted a humanitarian visa to return to the U.S. for medical treatment.

Of newer vets who had been here, one is in an alcohol program and the other is "running amok," Barajas-Varela says.

I'm not surprised. Deported veterans aren't angels. They have been convicted of serious and, in some cases, reprehensible offenses. I don't like some of them. That said, the punishment they received for their crimes went far beyond what a U.S. citizen would face for the same offense. Though in every way they had lived as Americans and even risked

---

In July 2016, the ACLU issued a report, "Discharged Then Discarded."

their lives for the U.S., they were banished from their homes after they were released from prison.

They got no second chance. Until now.

"I'll go see my daughter," Barajas-Varela tells me between bites of his breakfast. "I'll go straight to her. Surprise her at school. That'd be cool. I'm a little nervous. I think it's going to happen. I'll come to Tijuana once a month, see how everyone is doing here. I got to continue the work."

"I'm thinking of getting a degree in a public speaking," he continues. "Raise money for vets. Be a veterans' advocate. I can't re-up because of my record."

He gets reflective and reminisces about leaping out of airplanes when he served in the Eighty-Second Airborne Division. He was so scared every time he jumped. Four-second free fall. Then the chute opens automatically. But he was falling fast, so he would drop to the ground as soon as possible to avoid becoming a target. Each time, he anticipated a hard fall. Oh, shit, here it comes. Some guys landed standing up and didn't roll. They broke hips, ankles, everything.

These days, when Barajas-Varela sees people diving off cliffs into the ocean, he thinks they're crazy.

"I liked the military. Steady paycheck and all. Fuck, you're a soldier. You can retire at age forty. Wearing the uniform. Your buddies are studded with medals. Looks good."

However, he'll gladly accept civilian status living once more in the U.S.

Since interviewing most of the deported veterans in this book, my situation has changed too. I returned to the country club and worked another six-month season. Then in August 2015, I got a second chance. An editor I had worked with as a news reporter had been hired by *The National Catholic Reporter*. She called me one afternoon while I was cutting fairways. She needed writers, she said, and offered steady free-lance work. I stopped the mower, walked into the supervisor's office, and resigned. I was a reporter again. I never expected my own second chance. I tell Barajas-Varela about my new job but he doesn't hear me. He has other things on his mind.

"Some guys won't see anything any time soon if they have an aggravated felony on their record," he says. "Not everyone will get the chance Torres and I got. One guy applied for a humanitarian visa so he could be treated for PTSD. The visa wasn't granted. Mauricio. He saw the most combat of the guys here. Afghanistan. There's a difference between combat vets and the other guys."

He gets up to wash his plate. He has on a tank top, shorts, and flip-flops. He tells me there's bottled water by his bunk if I'm thirsty. I'm good, I say. In a moment he comes back from the kitchen, his hands wet from washing his dish.

"I don't want to be in Compton," Barajas-Varela says. He sits back at his desk. "I don't want to put myself in an en-vironment that might get me in trouble again. In Tijuana, I've endured the worst. I could disappear and use and who would know? I want to avoid that. To put myself in a situ-ation like that. I could relapse. I got to always work on it. Even once I'm a citizen, God willing. I don't want to go back to fucking jail."

Outside the Bunker's open door, I see a white compact sedan pull up and park. A lean man with glasses, blue jeans, and a green T-shirt gets out. He sees me and offers a slow smile. He speaks my name firmly but not loudly and grasps my hand.

"Daniel Torres," he says.

He greets Barajas-Varela. They speak Spanish. Barajas-Varela mentions his appointment in San Diego. He is giddy, laughing as he speaks. Torres nods and smiles.

"Barajas-Varela will make it," Torres tells me. We walk up a flight of stairs to the kitchen and sit at a round table. "Immigration is not going through all this, interviewing him and all that, for nothing," Torres says as we sit down. "I know in my heart he'll get it."

He pauses, stares at me. He has things on his mind, places he'd rather be. He hasn't seen his girlfriend in a few days. He's meeting her after we talk. He glances at his watch, looks back at me with a level gaze. I have the sense that he's sizing me up, determining whether or not I'm worth his time. Whether or not he should trust me.

I ask him where in Mexico he is from.

"Tijuana," he says.

He grew up in Lomas del Matamoros, one of the poorest neighborhoods. His home built from old garage doors, a one room shack with no walls dividing the kitchen from the bath. Cramped quarters for a family of five.

But everyone Torres knew lived like that. As a kid, he played kickball in the dirt streets. He had a job as a bagger at Giant Supermarket. He used the money to see movies, buy toys. His parents didn't give him money. He had to work.

His father worked in San Diego as a technician. He had a degree as an electrical engineer but his Mexican credentials meant nothing in the U.S. While he earned more than he would have in Mexico, it was not enough to move his family to San Diego. He left the house at dawn, and depending on the line at the border, arrived at work an hour and a half later.

After 9/11, his commute doubled to three hours and longer as security at the border increased. He now left the house on Mondays and stayed with friends in San Diego, returning to Tijuana late Friday night. Time passed but the lines remained long, so he told his family they might as well move to the United States.

But where? San Diego was expensive and Los Angeles was dirty and rife with gangs. Torres' godmother lived in Salt Lake City. She told his parents a lot of work was available in Utah. No gangs. A godly city of Mormons. His parents visited and liked what they saw. At 15, Torres helped the family pack up the house, load a van, and leave Tijuana. The family intended to return for the remainder of their meager possessions but they never bothered.

At first they lived with his godmother. He remembers he was surprised at all the street signs, at how clearly addresses were displayed outside houses. Tijuana had street names too, but no visible addresses. In Salt Lake City, all the streets had numbers and directions, east, west, north and south. Impossible to get lost. In Tijuana people say, Go to the corner, go two blocks, take another right and you'll find such-and-such street.

Torres pauses to answer his phone. His mother called, checking in. He also texts his girlfriend. Downstairs, I hear Barajas-Varela moving around, talking to someone. I hear his laugh, the excitement still in his voice. Torres puts his phone down.

Everyone was real nice in Salt Lake, he recalls. Neighbors knew each other. He felt a sense of community. The Torres family lived in a large town house. Nice. It had AC, a dishwasher, and a washing machine, comforts he had never experienced before.

"A convenient life," he says.

He did not miss Tijuana at all. His English was good from visits to San Diego on weekends but his accent was terrible. At school in Salt Lake everyone corrected him. But soon his pronunciation improved and he spoke English like any other American kid. After a while, he didn't see himself as different.

The subject of citizenship never came up. Torres attended school, applied for his driver's license, no problem. He grew up like any other American kid. He liked rock music, had a girlfriend. Deportation? He never even considered it a possibility. Utah was very tolerant. No one worried about his status.

Then he turned 18. He was considered an adult. His visa, issued to him as a dependent, was no longer valid. He could not work legally. He could not get student loans for college. With just a flip of the calendar, his world had become much smaller.

He looked into applying for citizenship but the advice he received left him few options. Immigration authorities told him he needed to leave the country and apply for residency from Mexico. But his friends told him if he did and his application was denied, he would not be allowed back into the country. And he would likely be denied, they said. He had no special skills, nothing the U.S. would consider an asset. No special visa existed for a high school graduate.

Torres got by with labor jobs supervised by businesses willing to pay him under the table. When he turned 21 in 2007, he ran into an old high school buddy, a recruiter for the Marines. He told Torres he had quotas to meet but no one was enlisting, especially in the infantry. The Iraq War was four years old, and that country had descended into chaos. He encouraged Torres to sign up. Torres agreed to enlist. Not because he saw the Marines as a path to citizenship, but because his life had been going nowhere for the past three years. He didn't know what else to do. But to join the Marines he needed ID. He had his Social Security card and a driver's license but no green card. Without it, he would need a fake U.S. birth certificate to enlist.

Torres walked to a nearby Mexican market, a convenience store where there was always a guy selling fake documents, standing outside, chilling. White people might think he was a dope dealer. But anyone from Mexico would know he was dealing fake documents.

Hey, Torres said, I need a birth certificate. Where can I get one? I have money. I need it to join the Marines.

Let me call a friend, the man said. He can make one. I do Social Security cards.

I have that.

Torres saved two months to raise the $250 to pay for the fake birth certificate. Once he had it, he walked to the recruiting office on a Monday to enlist. A gunnery sergeant was present to check the paperwork. When he took a break, Torres's buddy slid his documents through, an oh-this-one-too kind of thing.

You're going to Iraq, the recruiter told him.

Yeah, whatever, Torres said.

He wasn't nervous. He thought he knew what he was getting into. He liked video games. He could do Iraq. A dumb young man who thought he was invincible, that was him then, Torres says. There are two types of Marines: Stupid and crazy. He supposes he was a little of both.

Two days later, he flew to boot camp.

Torres spent three months in the Marine Corps recruit depot in San Diego. A different world. He came from well-mannered Salt Lake City, and in San Diego he had a bald side-of-beef drill sergeant screaming in his face. It was as if the man was unable to speak normally, that he had to shout out every single syllable to stress the hell out of the recruits. It was kind of like a brainwashing center indoctrinating young, impressionable men into the cult of war and the brotherhood of the Corps. It's pride. It's refusal to be defeated. It's refusal to surrender.

He bought into it. Hard not to. Even today, he'll meet a Marine and know without speaking a word. He checks the

guy out just as the guy is checking him out. They stop, intro-
duce themselves, ask where they served. They know. The look
in their eye, the way they carry themselves. A fellow Marine.
They know. Marines aren't the strongest or the fastest but what
sets them apart is they don't quit. They keep going. Being a
Marine is a state of mind. Marines first, that's the ideology.
They don't see themselves as soldiers. Soldiers are patriots.
God and country. Marines are all about Marines, the Corps.
Fighting to fight. Not everyone's cut out for it. In boot camp,
a recruit tried to kill himself. Threw himself off a four-story
building.

"You don't have to be crazy to be a Marine," Torres says,
"but it helps."

After he graduated from boot camp, Torres was assigned
to the First Battalion, Seventh Regiment. He spent another
six months in the States, training. He was the new guy, a
boot. The bottom of the ladder. He got the shit jobs: standing
watch, cleaning. Not until he deployed and returned would
he get respect. It sucked being a boot. Some guys couldn't
handle it. They went AWOL, attempted suicide, used drugs,
and got into fights.

Torres got his chance to prove himself when the Seventh
Regiment deployed to Iraq in February 2009. He wanted
to show he was good enough to be a Marine, that he was a
warrior. He wanted to fight, to use his weapon. He wanted
ribbons. He wanted to kill. It was what he had trained for,
sweated for, bled for, cried for. Combat. Without it, all he'd
been through it would be like attending school and not taking the final exam. He had a blood thirst.

The regiment spent two weeks in Kuwait with nothing
around but an empty, flat, white, sandy landscape. Iraq was
not any better. Iraq was shit. Iraq sucked balls. He spent three
months at Observation Post Castillo outside Fallujah. A

sixteen-man compound in fucking nowhere making sure no bad guys planted explosives on a dirt road used by the military and that no one drove more than twice a week. Six-hour shifts standing watch, staring at the desert. He went into full zombie mode and talked to himself to stay alert. What the fuck are we doing here? he'd think. I could be home. Instead, I'm watching a fucking road no one cares about. Lots of people think *Black Hawk Down* is what war is like. That was one battle. War's not like that 24/7.

At the end of May, the regiment moved to Observation Post Viking in Saqlawiyah, Iraq. He'd listen to the stories of Marines who had been in country when the war started. How they'd cut the enemy in half with an AK-47. How they'd blow up bad guys with grenades. Hard-core shit like that. But Torres didn't see war. Not like that. His regiment watched the fucking desert. They patrolled. Patrols were nerve-wracking, the vacant streets threatening in their silence. Marines who had been deployed before said an empty street usually meant insurgents planned to attack. But they never attacked. The Marines began turning more responsibility over to Iraqi soldiers and police.

Torres is unsparing in his criticism of them. They were weak, he says, stupid. They couldn't do three pushups. They didn't know how to do jumping jacks. They smoked weed and heroin. They were all smiles. They'd say what you wanted to hear. America good, shit like that, and then do what they wanted. The Marines would tell them to bring ten guys to this checkpoint. They would say, "God willing," and then not show up. Are you fucking serious, the Marines would ask themselves. They had no respect for the Iraqis.

At least the interpreters could be relied on, Torres says. The regiment had this Kuwaiti guy, an interpreter. He carried an AK-47. If the bad guys wanted to kill him, the Marines figured he was all right.

Torres and his regiment returned to the States in September 2009 to Twentynine Palms, California, in the middle of the Mojave Desert. It was given to the Marine Corps by the Army in the 1970s because it was considered uninhabitable. Marines were like, We can live here, Torres says. It sucked. Palm Springs was the closest town. They trained, worked out, played video games, and drank a lot on weekends in San Diego, Las Vegas, and LA. Torres felt unproven, disappointed. At home, what was he to do? Shoot someone to prove himself? No. He could do nothing. It sucked. People would say, oh, you've been to Iraq. You must have PTSD. No, Torres was just bored.

He signed up for a one-year deployment in Afghanistan for the 2010 surge. But then, one drunken night in Las Vegas, he lost his wallet and with it his military ID, driver's license, everything. He didn't have the necessary documents to get new ID and the Marines would require him to have those documents so they could be compared to the ones on file. If he used his real birth certificate, it would reveal he had been born in Mexico.

But you got my documents, Torres said.

It's protocol, Torres. We have to see yours.

With no other options, he told his commander he could not get his documents.

Get them in the mail, his commander said.

I can't. I wasn't born in the U.S.

You're a resident?

No.

You're illegal, Torres?

Yes.

How the fuck did you join?

I joined just like a citizen.

He could have faced fraud charges and a possible four-year prison sentence in a military prison. However, the

Marines did not file charges. He had a good service record and no criminal history. In 2011, he was given an honorable discharge under honorable conditions.

Figure out your life as a civilian, his commander told him.

"I felt like I had wasted four years of my life," Torres says, his voice flat from reliving that moment.

He had nothing. No job, no future. He was back to where he had started when he enlisted. With E-Verify, even under-the-table work would be hard to find. He decided to leave the U.S. He saw no future there. He was a military man, now. He was good at it. He scoured the web and decided to join the French Foreign Legion. He knew about them. Badasses. French mercenaries. He'd have to fly to Paris. He told his parents they'd see him in four or five years.

He stayed two weeks in Fort de Nogent, a French stockade forming part of the fortifications of Paris. He ran obstacle courses, ran timed runs. He did push-ups, sit-ups. He was fine. He was a Marine. He did what he was asked without breaking a sweat. But he had partial hearing loss in his left ear from weapons training as a Marine. That did him in. He failed the medical exam. Five hundred other guys were trying to join. The Legion chose the best. It didn't choose Torres. He was 25.

He returned to Tijuana. He had no idea where else to go. He was legal there even if he no longer felt like a Mexican.

"I self-deported," he says. Like fucking cold water, getting turned down by the Legion. He had no backup plan. He was living his life over, returning to the city he had left at 15.

He moved into an apartment owned by his grand-mother. He enrolled in The Autonomous University of Baja California in Tijuana and entered law school. He wanted to serve Mexico. He had gotten nowhere trying to serve the U.S. or France. He was very discouraged. He carried himself like

a Marine: cold, distant, irritable, angry. It took him a while
to climb out of that hole.

He met Barajas-Varela in 2014. At the time, Torres
thought, I'm the only soldier to serve and have to leave
the U.S. Then his uncle showed him a pamphlet about the
Deported Veterans Support House. His uncle was an ac-
countant at SIMNSA Hospital, a medical center that catered
to American citizens. Barajas-Varela had spoken at a benefit
party the day before. Torres's uncle told him about Torres.
Tell him to come by, Barajas-Varela said. Torres began volun-
teering at the Bunker. He liked being with other vets, around
guys in the same situation as himself.

That same year, the ACLU lawyers began their interviews
with Torres and other deported veterans. They made a report. They told Torres he was eligible for citizenship under
special provisions of the Immigration and Nationality Act
that allow for people who serve in the military during a period of hostility. It waives other usual requirements for citizenship, such as lawful permanent residence and physical
presence in the United States. They told him to fill out an
immigration application.

In December 2015, the ACLU submitted his citizenship
application to immigration officials. He received a visitor's
visa to take the test required of all prospective U.S. citizens
in San Diego. He thought he might get U.S. citizenship, but
he tried not to dwell on it. He didn't want to feel good and
then be disappointed.

On April 21, 2016, he crossed the border into San Diego. It
was very strange to enter the U.S. again after five years. Weird.
He was happy to cross but didn't want to get his hopes up. He
didn't want to go back to Tijuana. He took the citizenship test
at the U.S. immigration building in downtown San Diego. He
sat in a room with his attorney and an immigration official.

The official asked how he had enlisted, what he did after he left the Marines, what his future plans were, what political organizations he affiliated with if any, and if he had associated with terrorists. He answered questions for two hours.

We have all the information we need, the official told him. We'll do the oath in two hours.

He left the room. He'd done it. He would be a citizen. Torres felt beat, an exhaustion beyond description. He didn't know how to react. It had happened. He'd done it. He would be a citizen. He felt he was dreaming. He couldn't stop grinning like an idiot. He ate sushi for lunch and then returned to take the oath. After the brief ceremony, he returned to Tijuana. He had a class that afternoon.

Torres says he will finish university in Baja in June 2017. Then he will return to the States and prepare for the exam required to enter law school in the U.S. He'll apply to the University of Southern California, schools in San Diego, Salt Lake, maybe Denver, too.

"It has been a crazy ride. We can't choose where we were born, but we can choose who we are loyal to," Torres says.

He is loyal to the U.S. In Mexico, he saw corruption. This is how it is, people told him. It won't change. In the U.S people can do something, Torres tells me. People can still make a difference. He believes in the idea of America. The idea that anyone can participate in changing the system. That is freedom, he says. In Mexico, if you speak out you will be beaten, maybe killed, he says.

He stands up. He has a quiet assertiveness that is firm yet not aggressive. We've been talking for almost two hours, and now he's letting me know without saying a word that we're done. He's running late for his girlfriend.

I follow him downstairs to his car. Another vet, Erasmo Apodaca, a deported Marine, is talking to Barajas-Varela.

Torres says goodbye to them both, explains he can't stay. Torres and I shake hands and he offers me his half smile again. I walk him to the door.

"How long does a person have to pay for a mistake?" Torres says. "His entire life? Can they learn and value life? I have."

As I watch Torres get in his car, I hear Barajas-Varela ask Apodaca if he has filed for U.S. citizenship.

"Yeah, according to my lawyer."

"ACLU?"

"Yeah, Jenny Pasquarella."

"That's great."

"Send immigration my fingerprints and then take the test. Some of the guys are like, 'Fuck, I wish it was me.' I applied for citizenship between '03 and '08 twice but got turned down."

Apodaca tells me he served in Desert Storm from 1989 to 1992 and received an honorable discharge. He was deported in 1996 after he was convicted of residential burglary, an aggravated felony. He served fourteen months in Rosemond, California, near LA.

"I broke into an ex-girlfriend's house and stole some dresses," he tells Barajas-Varela.

"That's it?"

"Slashed her water bed, too. She was fucking someone else. I was pissed off, man. I went back to the U.S. in 2000 but I got caught and got deported again."

"I can't believe this fucking nightmare is almost over," Barajas-Varela says.

"What will you do?"

"Stay over there with my daughter and run this place. They might decide right there like they did with Daniel," Barajas-Varela says. "I can't wait. I hope they tell me that day. You stressed?"

"It has been fucking twenty years, Barajas-Varela. I'm used to this life."

"I'm stressed."

"If it happens, great."

"I'm not staying here," Barajas-Varela says.

I feel good listening to them, taking notes, resuming my life as a reporter again. Barajas-Varela asks me to take their photograph and gives me his iPad. He and Apodaca stand shoulder to shoulder. They stand straight. They adopt a stern, humorless look. The look, I imagine, of the fighting men they had once been or had envisioned themselves to be. An identity they still embrace despite their status, despite their own ruinous choices and those of U.S. lawmakers intent on showing their tough-on-illegal-immigration political bona fides. They are flawed men but soldiers still, as American as anyone in their units and just as proud.

Coming Home II

Facebook

November 15, 2016, 8:30 p.m.

Hector Barajas-Varela

Lately I've been praying a whole lot, preparing for the inter-view. Lord, grant me the opportunity to return to my daugh-ter. Friday, I hope to to take the oath for the last time to defend our constitution, my country America. I've taken this oath twice when I enlisted & re-enlisted.

My mistakes do not make me un-American, if anything my per-severance and persistence in spite of all obstacles, discourage-ments, and impossibilities, these also make me an American.

—Spc B Eighty-Second ABN Paratrooper life deportation from U.S.

U.S Army 95-2001 honorable discharge.

On November 18, 2016, the morning of his citizen-ship hearing, Hector Barajas-Varela wakes up and stares at the ceiling. He meets with U.S. immigration officials at nine. He has waited a long time for this moment. Too long. He will take a written and oral exam. The oral exam, he knows, will focus on his criminal record. That worries him. How much will his past be held against him? Will they understand he has changed?

The hearing should last about an hour and a half. Barajas-Varela has no idea what might happen. He is sleepy and excited, a bundle of nerves. He has not told his daughter about this day. He does not want to disappoint her if the decision goes against him.

He checks his phone for Facebook messages. He does not really pay attention to the notes wishing him good luck, his mind too cluttered with the civic questions he might be asked:

What happened at the Constitutional Convention?

Why did the colonies fight the British?

What does the Executive Branch do?

The night before on the phone, ACLU attorney Jennifer Pasquarella asked him once again about an alias he used when he crossed illegally into the United States after his first deportation. The alias was Hector Lopez. And what fake documents did you use? Social Security card and green card, he thought. He could not recall exactly. But he's pretty sure he had to buy a fake green card to work.

"I'd rather go in with the truth so they can't say I didn't," Barajas-Varela told Pasquarella.

"We'll get through this," she said.

"I'm dying here," Barajas-Varela said and laughed a laugh that was desperate and nervous in equal measure. Will a decision about his status be reached the same day as his interview? Will he have to wait? How long? Days, weeks, months? Pasquarella didn't know.

"Tomorrow, we'll celebrate or appeal," she told him. "We'll kick it to the courts if we have to. It's not the end of the road."

"I got to study."

"You're ready. Just be your genuine self."

"That's the problem sometimes," Hector said.

He laughed again. That pained laugh; full of worry and of hope.

"It's down to the wire," he said to himself as he got off the phone. He turned to a stack of papers and read for the umpteenth time questions he might be asked.

Who was president in World War One?

What does the Judicial Branch do?

He stretched out on the cot. He no longer slept in the bathroom he had converted into a bedroom. Now he was out in the middle of the front office. Bedbugs in some clothing donations he had stored in the bathroom had infiltrated his clothes and a couch. He had to spray everything, he told himself. Later. Now he needed to study. Answer questions about his past truthfully, he reminded himself. So no one can accuse him of being dishonest. The U.S. Citizenship and Immigration Manual states "an applicant for naturalization must show that he or she has been, and continues to be, a person of good moral character. In general, the applicant must show good moral character during the five-year period immediately preceding his or her application for naturalization and up to the time of the Oath of Allegiance."

Now, almost 12 hours after he lay on his cot and fell into a fitful sleep, he asks himself whether he has done enough to make up for past mistakes. Can anyone ever really do enough? It depends on who you ask, he supposes. On a Facebook post, he wrote, "personally I am not perfect but I have tried thru all obstacles, personal victories & mistakes to better myself & help others. I am a man of different thoughts, actions, and heart. Whatever they decide it will never change my status of being an all American U.S. veteran, my patriotism."

If he gets his citizenship, he'll go home for the weekend and then return to Tijuana. He has a deported veterans Thanksgiving dinner to plan. A mobile health clinic is coming to the Bunker for three days. In the past four months, more than 20 deported veterans contacted him for help. Emails and Facebook messages from guys in Peru, Juarez, Bolivia, the Dominican Republic. You name it. Citizenship or not, he does not see his obligations to these men ending any time soon.

What is freedom of religion?

What is the economic system in the U.S.?

What is the rule of law?

Barajas-Varela gets up. After a shower, he carries his black Army boots to a chair and polishes them. The shine reflects the growing light coming through the glass front door. He sticks his left hand inside each boot to stretch the leather so every crease gets rub downed from the stained rag in his hand. When he finishes, he places the boots on the floor and puts on his Army dress blues. He snaps the brass buttons closed around his chest, slips on his pants and tugs them around his waist. Not as thin as he was when he enlisted. He adjusts a red beret at a slight tilt on his head. He riffles through his briefcase. Passport? Yes. Birth certificate? Yes. Letters of support? Yes. He looks up, stands straight. He stares at himself in a mirror. Airborne all the way, he tells himself.

On a bus minutes later, he wipes perspiration from his forehead.

Name two rights everyone has in the United States.

He gets off the bus near la frontera, the border. People carrying bags and suitcases walk up ramps and through doors that will lead them into the United States. Vendors hawk piñatas and boys pushing carts of burritos and tacos call out to passersby. A deported Afghanistan War veteran with post-traumatic stress calls to Barajas-Varela. They hug. The vet wishes Barajas-Varela luck.

A deported, Vietnam War veteran leans on a cane approaches Barajas-Varela. They shake hands. More deported vets converge around Barajas-Varela, Marines and Army men, most of them with drug convictions, and he smiles and embraces each one.

"Thank you, Hector."

"Good luck, man."

"You'll be eating lunch at KFC soon."

Customers outside a nearby pharmacy stop and stare at the small gathering. Even at this early hour, a traffic jam exists at the border, and drivers waiting to enter the United States look out their windows at the man in the American Army uniform and the men gathered around him. Barajas-Varela tries to speak. His voice catches.

"Whatever happens, nothing will change in my heart," he says, the words breaking with his tears. "I love my family. I love my country. I love you guys. I will keep working to get you home. Airborne all the way!"

Barajas-Varela embraces all of them one more time and then walks toward the border. The veterans follow him.

"I hope he makes it," one says. "If they give it to him, it will change things for a lot of us."

The veterans watch Barajas-Varela pass through a gate flanked by two security guards. He takes a ramp to a border patrol office. Before he steps inside, he ponders the glinting skyline of San Diego. The sun shines. A bright blue day filled with a mix of uncertainty and possibility. Barajas-Varela opens the door. He does not look back.

Epilogue

Hector Barajas-Varela
Facebook
November 18, 2016, 4:22 p.m.

When I finished my interview, I actually had to go through the regular [walk] lanes when I came back into Mexico so I was in the U.S. territory in the outside offices for a couple of seconds. So, when I had to go back into the lines [to Mexico] and my attorney had to go the other way, I did shout, 'I made it!' So, I made it for three seconds. That was awesome. It felt good, it felt good to be on soil, U.S. soil for three seconds. So I made it three seconds. Airborne. It was beautiful.

In an April 3, 2017, Facebook video, Barajas-Varela told viewers that U.S. Citizenship and Immigration Services had yet to make a decision about his status. However, the agency had notified him that it was "considering denying me."

"I truly feel I'm an American in my heart," Barajas-Varela said, pausing between words, eyes wet. "I think I've paid my dues long and hard, that I've tried, really, really tried to become a better person, and I think it's time for me to go home."

Almost two weeks later, Barajas-Varela received very different news: On April 15, a day before Easter, California Governor Jerry Brown pardoned Barajas-Varela and two other deported veterans of the crimes that led to their deportation.

"I got a pardon from the governor of California and two other brothers got it," Barajas-Varela said on Facebook. "My God! This is huge. The process will be easier for me to go home to my family. I'm just very thankful."

On June 3, 2017, Representative Joaquín Castro of Texas led a delegation of Democrats, all members of the Hispanic Caucus, to meet Barajas-Varela and other deported veterans in Tijuana.

"What you see here today is a travesty," Castro said outside the Bunker. "Anyone willing to risk their life for the United States should not be subject to deportation."

In April 2015, the Third Circuit Court in Philadelphia court determined that the military conviction of Jose Chavez-Alvarez for sodomy was not a crime for which he was imprisoned at least one year, as called for by the 1996 immigration law, because he had received a general sentence for multiple offenses. The decision contained compelling language, declaring at one point that the government's case against Chavez-Alvarez "scarcely passes the laugh test."

He was released to the custody of his ex-wife. His travel is restricted. The Third Circuit Court referred his case back to the Board of Immigration Appeals.

Not far from the Bunker in Las Playas, Fabian Rebolledo stares at the mildewed walls of his living room. A movie plays, although he forgot its name as soon as he slipped the DVD into the player. He thought he was a citizen when he joined the Army. He thought it was automatic the minute he enlisted. He asked, am I a citizen?

Hey, don't worry, man, the recruiter said. You're a soldier. You don't need a visa or a residency card.

All right, man, Rebolledo said.

Some days, Alex Murillo sits in his Rosarito apartment and thinks back to his childhood in Phoenix. One time he overheard his mother talk about a cousin who had been deported. At the time he thought, that sucks, and then went out and played with his friends. He didn't dwell on it. He certainly never thought it would happen to him. As far as he was concerned, he was an American. Still feels that way. He served in the U.S. Navy. Saluted the flag. Be All You Can Be. Standing in front of a mirror at boot camp for the first time in his black-on-black night watch uniform. Wow. Look at him. His parents saw him graduate as an honor recruit. He was on his way. God and country. No one can take that feeling from him. His kids won't get deported. They are Americans. No one can take that away from him either.

On December 21, 2016, a Pennsylvania court threw out the aggravated felony charge against Neuris Feliz, saying the federal law defining the charge was too vague. As a consequence, Feliz has been cleared for a hearing to determine whether his deportation order should be dropped. Because of a backlog of immigration cases, he will have to wait until December 2017 for that hearing. While he waits, Feliz dreams. He dreams alone. He and his wife divorced. Sometimes he dreams about prison. More often, he dreams about Iraq. He is in his barracks when *Boom!* Boom! Mortars explode, or, he sees himself on guard duty escorting cars into the concrete box.

He has a packet of photos in a plastic bag. Photos of exploded bodies, traces of blood, brains, burned vehicles. An Army buddy, an infantry soldier, took them and gave them to him. They're memories, Feliz said. He doesn't look at them and go crazy. They're just there. In a desk drawer.

He does not miss Iraq. He misses the Army. The discipline, the competence. The Army is very organized compared to the civilian world. The civilian world is so different. It's tough to get used to the civilian world. Where's the discipline, the organization? In the Army, everything is done one way. Period. It's not going to change. He found acceptance in the Army. People looked up to him. No, he doesn't miss Iraq, but he misses the Army.

His mind wanders. He leafs through his tattered prison journal, holding it like a precious old book that he picked up somewhere in another time. In the solitude of his cell, he had reflected on the war and that day in April 2004 when he first saw injured soldiers.

I remember a guy I was treating for a wounded foot. He had an entrance and an exit wound. The bullet went in his lower right ankle and came out on the upper left side of his ankle. I grabbed my Combat Lifesaver Bag and reached for my bandage. I wrapped it around his ankle and applied plenty of pressure to stop the bleeding. I looked to my right side and there was my friend Leslie Denise Jackson. She told me, "I didn't join for this." I looked back at her and nodded. I got back on my feet and looked around. It took me a few minutes to completely digest the madness surrounding me. There were several wounded soldiers on the ground. I saw many of them holding pictures of their loved ones, their eyes filled with tears. Tears of pain, but not pain from their wounds. It was pain coming from their hearts. Beside me was a man struggling to breathe. Struggling for his life. And he just died. It was the first time I ever saw someone die, right there before my eyes. Things weren't the same after that. They would never be the same.

Alberto Garcia intends to write a letter to all the living U.S. presidents and ask their forgiveness. I was trying to do my best for my country and as far as I know I did it, he'll say. I regret I did something wrong. It was my first crime. And now, Mr. President, I'm being treated as a criminal for the rest of my life.

Cesar Lopez hopes to leave Las Vegas for northern California. Or maybe he'll go overseas. All that effort to get home and now he's thinking about leaving the country. Crazy, huh? But he wants to get the jump on immigration before they throw him out again. That bad feeling of his days being numbered stays with him. Screw going to Mexico and opening a restaurant. Maybe Costa Rica again. No, not Costa Rica. Costa Rica, like Texas, is bad luck. No matter what country he chooses, he can't return if he leaves.

He doesn't like that. The not returning part.

On November 3, 2016, Alberto Segura received a four year prison sentence for driving under the influence, after which he could face deportation hearings. His wife, Olivia Segura, said he wants to get involved in a program for alcoholics. She's still angry at him, but admits that she misses him every day. She wants to slap him with one hand and hold him with the other.

Her job has notified her that she will be laid off in four weeks. She may not be able to maintain her monthly car payments. She worries immigration officials will seek to deport Alberto after he serves his sentence.

"I need to move on with my life," she says.

But one day to the next, she doesn't know how she'll feel or what to expect.

Hans Irizarry does not want to die in the Dominican Republic but he suspects that he might. He saves his money and recently bought a kitchen stove. Beats the hell out of the little electrical hotplate he had.

He still gets depressed. A few times he has called a suicide hotline in the States. Once he explained that he had been deported. The voice on the other end said he could do nothing for him. Sorry. If you feel like talking again, call us.

He misses cold weather. The first day of snow. It looks so beautiful. All the snow in the trees. Here in the Dominican Republic, he feels trapped inside someone else's body. His mind is elsewhere but his body is here. He can describe what he's thinking but the people here don't understand. They've not seen it. They can't envision it. He thinks, fuck, I'm not home, and then everything inside him dies.

He doesn't belong here.

Acknowledgements

My deepest thanks to all the veterans at home and abroad who gave me their stories and so much of their time. And to attorneys Craig Shagin, Valerie Burch and Troy Mattes for first introducing me to the issue of deported veterans and for their patience with my many questions.

I especially want to thank the editors of Guernica: A Magazine of Art & Politics, Tampa Review, Latterly Magazine and The Massachusetts Review for first publishing some of these stories.

Jesse Barker, Ben Wolford, Roland Sharrillo, Joanne Beck Fish, and Chuck Murphy read early drafts of these stories and often read them more times than any one person should. I can not thank you all enough for your wise critiques.

Heather World kindly took on the ungrateful task of proofreader and scold. You put up with my impatience and nerves. My thanks to you for your friendship and for taking this on and for your patience.

To all the staff at Skyhorse Publishing, especially Caroline Russomanno and Mark Gompertz, my sincere thanks for considering this manuscript and welcoming me into your fold. I also need to thank former Skyhorse editor Jerrod MacFarlane for taking on this project and for his patience and encouragement.

Sandy Weiner Mattson, her daughter Emily and house-mate Jean kindly put me up in San Diego on my many travels to the Bunker in Tijuana. Many thanks for your hospitality. It was wonderful to see you again, Sandy, after so long.

My thanks also to Scott Canon, Stella Ferrer and Dale Maharidge for their encouragement on this effort and so many others, and as always to Molly Giles for your inspiration and restraint with my first pained efforts at story telling. And to the memory of David Littlejohn, Dale M. Titler and my brother Charles A. Garcia, Jr., each of you still my mentors and guiding lights.

I want to thank my former colleagues at the Ozanam Center and Hospitality House in San Francisco and to the homeless men and women I once worked with there. All of you encouraged my first hesitant steps toward storytelling and influenced my approach to reporting. I carry you with me always.

Finally, my love and profound gratitude to Olga Contreras for everything you gave me and that you continue to give me despite your absence. Before you died, you told me, "Don't look back, unless it's to gather a happy memory and smile." You're gone and I look back all the time now. There are no words.